OXFORD
INDIA SHORT
INTRODUCTIONS
TRADE AND
ENVIRONMENT

The Oxford India Short
Introductions are concise,
stimulating, and accessible guides
to different aspects of India.
Combining authoritative analysis,
new ideas, and diverse perspectives,
they discuss subjects which are
topical yet enduring, as also
emerging areas of study and debate.

A part of the *Oxford India Short Introductions* series, this book belongs to a cluster of nine titles around the theme 'Economics and Development'. I have deliberately kept these two words separate. We tend to forget that the non-economic aspects of development have an important bearing on the economic aspects. The focus of the theme is how a country like India faces and solves (or fails to solve) various questions related to its quest for sustainable development. Moreover, every book within this cluster presents the reader with a quick recapitulation of the relevant theory so that opinions can be disentangled from conclusions based on theory.

**Anindya Sen**, Professor of Economics, Indian Institute of Management Kolkata; General Editor for the cluster on 'Economics and Development', *OISI*

### *Other Titles in the Cluster*

**Indian Cities**
*Annapurna Shaw*

**Monetary Policy**
*Partha Ray*

**Capital Flows and Exchange Rate Management**
*Soumyen Sikdar*

OXFORD
INDIA SHORT
INTRODUCTIONS

# TRADE AND ENVIRONMENT

RAJAT ACHARYYA

**OXFORD**
UNIVERSITY PRESS

# OXFORD
UNIVERSITY PRESS

Oxford University Press is a department of the University of Oxford.
It furthers the University's objective of excellence in research, scholarship,
and education by publishing worldwide. Oxford is a registered trademark of
Oxford University Press in the UK and in certain other countries

Published in India by
Oxford University Press
YMCA Library Building, 1 Jai Singh Road, New Delhi 110 001, India

© Oxford University Press 2013

The moral rights of the author have been asserted

First Edition published in 2013

ISBN-13: 978-0-19-807542-4
ISBN-10: 0-19-807542-1

Typeset in 11/15.6 Bembo Std
by Excellent Laser Typesetters, Pitampura, Delhi 110 034
Printed in India at G.H. Prints Pvt Ltd, New Delhi 110 020

# Contents

# Tables, Figures, and Boxes

## Tables

## Figures

## Boxes

# Preface

Since the Second World War, world trade has increased phenomenally, both in quantum and in composition of the commodity trade basket. Income growth, technological advent, and innovation have all led to the development of new products and the expansion of the consumption basket. Population growth in developing countries has, on the other hand, put pressure on their natural resources to meet the growing and diversifying needs of consumption. Consequently, they have become increasingly dependent on imports to bridge the gap between their domestic consumption needs and local supplies. Trade barriers across the globe have also steadily declined over the last couple of decades, as a consequence of countries integrating with the global economy, either through unilateral trade liberalization or through regional trading arrangements. Thus, protectionism during the 1960s and 1970s has turned into the wave of globalization in the last two decades. These developments have further augmented the volume and dimensions of world trade.

Increased world trade, in turn, has fed into further growth in income, though not uniformly in different regions, propelling expansion of production activities globally. This spiralling growth–production–trade relationship is continuously putting pressure on the environmental resources of countries, as well as common property resources such as the oceans and the atmosphere. Whereas environmental degradation has raised major concerns amongst environmentalists, economists, policymakers, and international agencies alike, cross-country variations in environmental regulations, standards, and the level of pollution abatement have become a bone of contention amongst the developed and the developing nations. Environmental regulations imposed by developed countries on imports from developing countries have raised further concerns in developing nations as these measures often appear to be non-tariff barriers in disguise.

This book intends to introduce readers to the issues related to international trade and the environment that have been debated amongst economists and policymakers, and shaped much of the trade relations between the developed and the developing countries. While the discussions will, in general, be put in the broader perspectives of world trade, case studies on India and other countries will be used as exemplification of these issues.

The book draws heavily from different survey papers as well as my own research in the recent past with some of my co-researchers and students, particularly Kalyan K. Sanyal and Anindita Sen. My ideas have also been cleaned up by students at the Utrecht School of Economics while teaching trade and environmental issues in a post-graduate course during Spring 2010.

My special thanks go to Anindya Sen, General Editor for the cluster on 'Economics and Development', in the *Oxford India Short Introductions* series for suggesting changes in the presentation and content of this book. Above all, I cannot but gratefully remember the support I have received from my family—Joysri, Rajarshi, and Ritwik.

March 2013                               RAJAT ACHARYYA

# 1

# Trade and the Environment: General Issues

The link between international trade and the environment has been an area of extensive research and debate over the last two decades. Positive trade theorists have primarily been concerned with the question of how the environmental factor influences the pattern of comparative advantage and, thereby, the pattern of international division of labour. Those concerned with normative issues have focused on the welfare consequences of environmental costs, and explored the welfare effects of different policies. The second set of issues concerns the question of how environmental regulations influence the location of foreign investments. The third set of issues centres around the concept of the environment as a common global resource.

The major concern here is: what possible institutional arrangements can be made through which optimal utilization of the common resource can be ensured.

Here we discuss some of the general issues that set the perspectives of analyses in the chapters that follow.

## Two-way Causation

There are two possible ways in which the environment and international trade may be related. Larger volumes of international trade may cause pollution and environmental damage depending on the pattern of trade. On the other hand, undervaluation of the environment through lax implementation of the environmental standards and regulations can provide a basis for trade thereby establishing a reverse causation. Thus, the link between trade and the environment is not unidirectional, it is rather two-way.

International trade may affect the environment in many ways. Environmental damage can be caused through altering the production pattern and the technique. The increased export of industrial goods, for example, spurs industrial production, which in turn, degrades the environment in the form of air pollution. More factories are being set up, and production is increased in each of the existing ones to meet the demand for these goods from abroad under free trade. This rise in industrial production implies pollution of the fresh air through increased emissions of smoke and other suspended particulate matters. Similarly, the increased export of chemicals and pharmaceuticals causes larger dumping of wastes in the water, thereby, polluting rivers and other sources of pure drinking water. Tanneries are another typical source of environmental degradation in the form of water pollution. The intense production of leather manufacture in existing and new tanneries as a consequence of India's increased exports of such items raises water pollution. The usage of chemical fertilizers to increase crop yields per acre so as to meet the rising export supply may exacerbate the toxic content of both the soil and crops, with consequent health hazards. Imports, however, may lower environmental degradation in the importing country to the extent to which it displaces the domestic production of pollutants or *dirty* goods like iron and steel, paper and pulp, chemicals, leather manufacture, rubber products, mineral production, wood products, ferrous and non-ferrous metals, and the like. This dimension of freer trade affecting the environment will be discussed in Chapter 2.

Income growth caused by free trade can also affect the environment. However, as shall be discussed later, this growth effect of free trade is usually beneficial for the environment since income growth results in a higher demand for better environmental quality (such as cleaner air and drinking water) which, in turn, induces the local governments to set higher environmental standards for domestic producers and implement pollution abatement rules more strictly. These further implications of freer trade through growth will be discussed in Chapter 3.

On the other hand, undervaluation of the environment in an economy can spur exports leading to a reverse causation. The absence of environmental regulation on industrial production enables its producers to charge prices less than the social cost of production—costs that production of the good inflicts on the rest of the economy in terms of health hazards. This may provide the country with a competitive edge in the international market as producers there undermine the true cost, and therefore, edge out the other country where such regulations exist and are strictly implemented—if other determinants of comparative advantage, such as technology, factor endowment, and tastes, are the same across nations. This type of comparative advantage is fundamentally different as it is a reflection of an underestimation of (social) cost. *It is a perverse, rather than genuine, comparative advantage.* In Chapter 5, a more elaborate discussion on this aspect of pollution havens hypothesis (which postulates that countries with weaker environmental regulations are the exporters of the relatively pollution-intensive goods) will be made.

What is worthwhile to mention here is that the comparative advantage of the developing countries per se does not reflect weak environmental standards there for two reasons. First, the comparative advantage is essentially a reflection of interaction amongst the fundamentals—factor endowment, technology, and tastes—and, of course, policy differences. Second, these fundamentals are not identical across developing and developed countries (see Box 1). On the other hand, a far-reaching implication of this interaction effect on the pattern of comparative advantage of nations is that advantages in factor endowment or in technology (or both) may overcome the cost disadvantage of stricter

## Box 1   Comparative Advantage

In a world of two commodities, leather bag and rice, a country has a comparative advantage in rice if its price relative to that of leather is lower in that country than abroad. Such a comparative advantage means through arbitrage—buying cheap and selling dear—rice will be exported and leather manufacture will be imported by this country. When prices are cost determined—such as when production costs are constant and all markets are perfectly competitive—comparative advantage essentially follows from comparative *cost* advantage. In propounding his Doctrine of Comparative Cost Advantage, David Ricardo (1817) emphasized that the cross-country differences in the production methods (or technologies) establish comparative *cost* advantage of one country over the other in production of goods.

environmental standards. Thus, countries with strict regulations may even export pollution-intensive goods.

## Unfair Trade and Ecological Dumping

The argument that weak environmental standards in the developing countries may establish their comparative advantage in environment-intensive dirty goods has become the bone of contention for the developed countries and has led to fierce debates at the World Trade Organization (WTO). In such debates, developed countries are in favour of imposing uniform standards across the globe so that genuine competitiveness, according to the fundamentals like productivity, can determine the pattern of trade. Developing countries, on the other hand, oppose this proposal as they see it as nothing but an attempt to use environmental issues as rationalization for non-tariff barriers for protecting the Northern domestic market from foreign competition. The production of dirty goods that pollute the environment generates a negative externality—costs that are inflicted upon the society but are not internalized by the private agents—and, consequently, the private cost of production remains far below the social cost of production. Lax environmental standards on the production of such goods, therefore, allow the producers to charge prices below the social marginal costs. The bone of contention centres on this ecological dumping that is due to non-inclusion of environmental costs into prices.

7

Two related issues have surfaced in the debate in this context. First, capital moves from countries where environmental regulations are stricter to those where these are loosely implemented. This is known as the capital flight hypothesis whereby dirty industries migrate to the developing nations. Second, developing and low-income countries are pollution havens. These countries deliberately keep their environmental standards low to attract capital from the richer ones. This often leads to race-to-the-bottom as developing countries compete among themselves to attract foreign capital. Chapter 4 will elaborate on the empirical evidence in this regard, and will contest the capital flight hypothesis. The other dimension of the discussions in this chapter is whether and how the inflow of foreign direct investment (FDI) per se degrades the environment in the host country.

There is some evidence that dirty goods are growing faster in the developing countries and the share of these goods in aggregate production is declining in the developed countries. This implies that dirty goods are indeed migrating (see Box 2). However, whether or not this is caused by weak environmental standards in developing countries remains a debatable issue.

Similarly, there is no prima facie evidence on direct foreign investment in these countries flowing primarily into the dirty industries. In several cases, FDI inflow is also found to be better for the local environment. We will return to this discussion in a latter chapter.

## The Taxonomy of Environmental Degradation or Pollution

Economic activities spurred by increased trade degrade the environment in more than one way. Both production and consumption of commodities may cause environmental degradation. For some commodities, pollution emission and other environmental damages are confined either to the production stage or to the consumption stage. It is, therefore, important to distinguish between such cases of production and consumption pollution. This is because whether or not international trade degrades the environment is essentially related to the question: at which stage pollution is emitted and the environmental damages are caused. If it is a case of production pollution, exports of dirty goods by developing countries to developed countries actually shifts pollution from the latter group of countries

## Box 2   Dirty and Clean Industries

There are many criteria for identifying dirty industries. By emissions intensity, that is, actual emissions per unit of output, rather than abatement costs, the five most pollution intensive industries are iron and steel, non-ferrous metals, industrial chemicals, pulp and paper, and non-metallic minerals. The five cleanest industries, on the other hand, are textiles, non-electrical machinery, electrical machinery, transport equipment, and instruments. Table 1 reports ranking of 10 most pollution intensive manufacturing industries in the USA in 1995.

to the former. The opposite, however, is the case when it is the consumption rather than the production of the traded good that degrades the environment.

This distinction between the nature of pollution—production or consumption—and the consequent nature of externality is important for several other reasons. First, the nature of optimal policy intervention would not be the same in both the cases. If pollution is generated while the goods are being produced rather than consumed, a socially optimal intervention requires a production tax or regulation. Otherwise, a consumption tax would be the optimal one. Second, in case of production pollution, a trade sanction by the Northern countries on imports of dirty goods from their Southern counterparts would shift pollution from the latter to the former. This is because the domestic production of the dirty good in Northern countries replaces imports from Southern countries. Once we understand this, it is difficult to rationalize the imposition of trade sanctions, and these surface as merely non-tariff barriers as is often alleged by the Southern countries.

Environmental degradation caused by production activities may also adversely impact other spheres of the production economy. In that case, the cost of pollution, apart from the direct loss of utility suffered by the society, makes itself felt as a loss of productivity in other sectors of production. A typical example would be the ashes emitted during industrial production which erode soil fertility when deposited again on the surface of the soil through rain. This would, therefore, have an adverse effect on crop productivity. The interesting aspect of such *cross effect* is that international trade may actually lower the magnitude of pollution rather than magnify it.

**TABLE 1** Ranking of the US Pollution-intensive Manufacturing Industries (1995)

| | Air | Water | Metals | Overall |
|---|---|---|---|---|
| 1 | Iron and Steel | Iron and Steel | Non-Ferrous Metals | Iron and Steel |
| 2 | Non-Ferrous Metals | Non-Ferrous Metals | Iron and Steel | Non-Ferrous Metals |
| 3 | Non-Metallic Mineral Production | Pulp and Paper | Industrial Chemicals | Industrial Chemicals |
| 4 | Miscellaneous Petroleum & Coal Production | Miscellaneous Manufacturing | Leather Products | Petroleum Refinery |
| 5 | Pulp and Paper | Industrial Chemicals | Pottery | Non-Metallic Mineral Production |
| 6 | Petroleum Refinery | Other Chemicals | Metal Products | Pulp and Paper |
| 7 | Industrial Chemicals | Beverages | Rubber Products | Other Chemicals |
| 8 | Other Chemicals | Food Products | Electrical Products | Rubber Products |
| 9 | Wood Products | Rubber Products | Machinery | Leather Products |
| 10 | Glass Products | Petroleum Refinery | Non-Metallic Mineral Production | Metal Products |

*Source*: Mani and Wheeler (1998).

Box 3   Air and Water Pollution in India

According to the World Health Organization (WHO), out of India's 3,119 towns and cities, only 209 have partial treatment facilities, 8 have full wastewater treatment facilities, 114 cities dump untreated sewage, and partially cremated bodies directly into the Ganges. Downstream, the untreated water is used for drinking, bathing, and washing. This situation is typical of many rivers in India as well as in other developing countries. A joint study by the Post Graduate Institute of Medical Education and Research (PGIMER) and the Punjab Pollution Control Board in 2008 revealed that, in villages along the Buddha Nullah—a rivulet which runs through the Malwa region of Punjab and after passing through highly populated Ludhiana district, drains into Sutlej River—calcium, magnesium, fluoride, mercury, beta-endosulphan and heptachlor pesticide were beyond the permissible limit in ground and tap waters. The water also had a high concentration of chemical oxygen demand (COD) and biochemical oxygen demand (BOD), ammonia, phosphate, chloride, chromium, arsenic, and chlorpyrifos pesticide. The ground water contains nickel and selenium, while the tap water has a high concentration of lead, nickel and cadmium.

(*contd...*)

Box 3 (*contd...*)

Indian cities are polluted by vehicles and industry emissions. Road dust due to vehicles also contributes up to 33 per cent of air pollution. The Central Pollution Control Board has identified iron and steel, thermal power plants, copper/zinc/aluminum smelters, cement, and oil refineries as highly air polluting industries. Pollution from different types of cooking stoves using coal, fuel wood, and other biomass fuels contributes to some extent, to the overall pollution load in urban areas.

The adverse impact of economic activities on the environment might be local, trans-boundary, and global in character. Economic activities may pollute and degrade the environment of a particular locality where such activities are undertaken, and remain confined there without having any trans-border effect. On the other hand, these activities may cause degradation of the global environment, affecting adversely the areas far off, and transmitting pollution from one country to another. This distinction is equally important as in the latter case national environmental policies, unless coordinated across the countries, are not enough to

## Box 4 Environmental Damages from Iron
Ore Mining in India

The most significant environmental damages due to iron ore mining in India are the deterioration of forest ecology, the alteration of land use pattern and changes in the local drainage system due to inadequate landscape management during mining operations, and improper and inadequate rehabilitation strategy adopted. As reported in the *Comprehensive Industry Document on Iron Ore Mining* published by the Central Pollution Control Board (New Delhi) in 2007, there has been a serious concern regarding the management and rehabilitation of the wastes and overburdened dumps. It has been observed by many researchers that ecological principles were not taken into account while carrying out the rehabilitation of mined out areas and waste rock dumps in the reserved forest areas. Current rehabilitation is principally directed at restoring visual amenity, stabilizing disturbed areas, and growing trees that will prove useful to the future generations. Rehabilitation practices for reserved forests, while also meeting these objectives, should aim to restore the native forest in all its diversity. Restoration of the forest vegetation, on the other hand, requires re-establishment of all forest components, not just trees.

achieve the globally optimum emission reduction or pollution abatement.

Moreover, in several cases of trans-boundary and global pollution, it is difficult to identify the polluter and the polluted, thereby adding another dimension to the problem of policy coordination. This is because trans-boundary pollution and the consequent externalities may be of different types and nature—unidirectional, regional reciprocal, and global externalities. The former takes place in instances where a river flows through more than one country on the same land mass. Here, production activities in an upstream country adversely affect the ecology of a downstream country. Regional reciprocal externality arises when there is a common property resource with free access for many countries. The European atmosphere as a dump for emissions from fossil fuel and consequent acid rain is a typical example. In the former example of unidirectional trans-boundary pollution, it is easy to identify the upstream country as the polluter and the downstream country as the polluted. This creates scope for applying the 'polluter pays principle'. However, in case of regional reciprocation trans-boundary pollution (or global externality), all countries in the region contribute to the degradation of the atmosphere, and are also affected by such degradation. It is difficult to identify to what extent each country is affected by its own emission and to what extent by emission of others. A more elaborate discussion on this issue is presented in Chapter 6.

## History of Trade and Environmental Issues at the GATT and the WTO

The first documentation of trade-related environmental concerns in the multilateral trade negotiation forum was the study entitled 'Industrial Pollution Control and International Trade' by the Secretariat of the General Agreement on Tariffs and Trade (GATT) in 1971 in preparation for the Conference on the Human Environment in Stockholm held by the United Nations in 1972. It reflected the concern of trade officials that linking environmental regulations to trade negotiations could pose obstacles to trade as well as constitute a new form of protectionism, which they termed 'green protectionism'.

In November 1971, the GATT Council of Representatives agreed to set up a Group on Environmental

Measures and International Trade, known as the 'EMIT' group, which would be open to all GATT members (that is, GATT signatories). However, the EMIT group would only convene at the request of GATT members, and it was not until 1991 when the members of the European Free Trade Association (EFTA) asked for the EMIT Group to be convened. The then EFTA included Austria, Finland, Iceland, Liechtenstein, Norway, Sweden, and Switzerland. So since its inception, the EMIT was inactive for as long as 20 years.

Between 1971 and 1991, environmental policies began to have an increasing impact on trade, and with increasing trade flows, the effects of trade on the environment had also become more widespread. During the Tokyo Round of trade negotiations (1973–9), participants deliberated on the degree to which environmental measures in the form of technical regulations and standards could hinder trade. The Tokyo Round Agreement on Technical Barriers to Trade (TBT), also known as the 'Standards Code', was negotiated. Amongst other things, it called for non-discrimination in the preparation, the adoption, and the application of technical regulations and standards. Transparency in such technical regulations and standards was also sought for.

During the Uruguay Round (1986–94), modifications were made to the TBT Agreement, and certain environmental issues were addressed in the General Agreement on Trade in Services, the Agreements on Agriculture (AoA), Sanitary and Phytosanitary Measures (SPS) (see Box 5), Subsidies and Countervailing Measures, and Trade-Related Aspects of Intellectual Property Rights (TRIPS). Quite a few developing countries expressed concerns about the lack of information on products prohibited in developed countries on the grounds of environmental hazards, health, or safety reasons. As a consequence, exports by the developing countries were largely being affected. At the 1982 GATT ministerial meeting, members decided to examine the measures needed to bring under control the export of products prohibited domestically (on the grounds of harm to human, animal, plant life or health, or the environment). This led to the creation of a Working Group on the Export of Domestically Prohibited Goods and Other Hazardous Substances in 1989.

The conflicting interests of environmental protection and trade liberalization came into prominence in 1991 with a dispute between Mexico and the United States. The case concerned a US embargo on tuna imported from Mexico that were caught using 'purse seine' nets which caused the incidental killing of dolphins. Mexico appealed to GATT on the grounds that the embargo was inconsistent with the rules of international trade. The ruling in favour of Mexico raised major concerns among environmental groups as it was felt that trade rules were an obstacle to environmental protection.

At the environmental forum, important developments were also taking place side by side in the context of the relationship between economic growth, social development, and the environment. In 1987, for example, the World Commission on Environment and Development produced the *Brundtland Report* entitled *Our Common Future*. This report coined the term 'sustainable development'. The report identified poverty as one of the most important causes of environmental degradation, and argued that greater economic growth, fuelled in part by increased international trade, could generate the necessary resources to combat the 'pollution of poverty'.

In accordance with its mandate of examining the possible effects of environmental protection policies on the operation of the General Agreement, the EMIT group focused on the effects of environmental measures (such as eco-labelling schemes) on international trade. The group also examined the relationship between rules of the multilateral trading system and trade provisions contained in the multilateral environmental agreements (MEAs). These MEAs include the Basel Convention on the Trans-boundary Movement of Hazardous Wastes.

The Rio 'Earth Summit' or the UN Conference on Environment and Development (UNCED) in 1992 stressed on the role of international trade in poverty alleviation and in combating environmental degradation. Among the programme of action adopted at the conference, it also addressed the importance of promoting sustainable development through international trade.

Towards the end of the 1986–94 Uruguay Round, the importance of working towards sustainable development was again reiterated in the preamble to Establishing the World Trade Organization, in the

Marrakesh Agreement in April 1994. It stated that WTO members should recognize 'that their relations in the field of trade and economic endeavour should be ... allowing for the optimal use of the world's resources in accordance with the objective of sustainable development'. Trade relations should protect and preserve the environment in a manner consistent with respective needs and concerns of the trading nations at different levels of economic development (see Box 6).

In Marrakesh, in April 1994, ministers also signed a 'Decision on Trade and Environment' which states that:

> There should not be, nor need be, any policy contradiction between upholding and safeguarding an open, non-discriminatory and equitable multilateral trading system on the one hand, and acting for the protection of the environment, and the promotion of sustainable development on the other.

The creation of the Committee on Trade and Environment was also felt to achieve several objectives. First, rules for trade and environmental measures, for the promotion of sustainable development, should take into consideration the needs of developing countries,

## Box 5 Sanitary and Phytosanitary Measures Agreement (SPS)

This is an agreement on food safety and animal and plant health standards. Food safety measures relate to bacterial contaminants, pesticides, inspection, and labelling. It allows countries to set their own standards, but these regulations must be based on science. These should be applied only to the extent 'necessary to protect human, animal or plant life or health', and should not 'arbitrarily or unjustifiably discriminate between countries where identical or similar conditions prevail'.

There have been quite a few cases of international conflicts. In 1996, European Union (EU) directives that prohibited the import and sale of meat and meat products treated with certain growth hormones was challenged by the US and Canada in the WTO Dispute Settlement Body (DSB), alleging that these directives violated several provisions of the SPS Agreement. The EU contended that the presence of the banned hormones in food may present a risk to consumers' health. As such, the directives were justified under several WTO provisions that authorize the adoption of trade-restrictive measures to protect human health. Further, in 2003, the US challenged a number of EU laws restricting the import of Genetically Modified Organisms (GMOs).

in particular those of the least developed. Second, protectionist trade measures should be discouraged and the multilateral trading system should be used to achieve environmental objectives set forth in Agenda 21 and the Rio Declaration.

Finally, there are the issues of climate change, which is now the biggest sustainable development challenge for the international community. It is a challenge that transcends borders, and requires solutions not only at national levels but at the international or supranational level as well. Though the issue of climate change per se is not part of the WTO's work programme, it is relevant because climate change measures and policies intersect with international trade in a number of different ways. Most important is that national measures to mitigate and adapt to climate change may modify conditions of competition and hence may have an impact on international trade. The WTO rules can be relevant, therefore, to the examination of climate change measures. Moreover, WTO rules, as a whole, offer a framework for ensuring predictability, transparency, and the fair implementation of such measures.

# Environmental Performance Index

The Environmental Performance Index (EPI) constructed by the Yale Center for Environmental Law & Policy, Yale University, and Center for International Earth Science Information Network, Columbia University, in collaboration with World Economic Forum and Joint Research Centre (European Commission), is a reflection of how countries implement their environmental policies and achieve their goals. It ranks 163 countries on 25 performance indicators across 10 policy categories that cover both environmental public health and ecosystem vitality. These indicators provide an indication of how close countries are to their respective established environmental policy goals. Table 2 reports the policy categories.

The proximity-to-target methodology of the EPI facilitates cross-country comparisons. Table 3 below reports the 2012 EPI for selected countries. The strongest performers are mostly from Europe whereas the weak performers (having EPI scores ranging between 39 and 49) are the countries mainly from Africa and Asia. India is ranked 125th amongst 132 countries with a very low score of 36.23.

**TABLE 2** Objectives, Policy Categories and Sub-categories, and Indicators

| OBJECTIVE | ENVIRONMENTAL HEALTH | | |
|---|---|---|---|
| Policy Categories | Environmental Burden of Disease | Water (effects on humans) | Air Pollution (effects on humans) |
| Indicators | Environmental Burden of Disease | Adequate Sanitation, Drinking Water | Indoor Air Pollution, Urban Particulates, Local Ozone |

| OBJECTIVE | ECOSYSTEM VITALITY | | |
|---|---|---|---|
| Policy Categories | Air Pollution (effects on ecosystems) | Water (effects on ecosystems) | Biodiversity and Habitat |
| Indicators | Regional Ozone, Sulfur Dioxide Emissions | Water Quality Index, Water Stress | Conservation Risk Index, Effective Conservation, Critical Habitat Protection, Marine Protected Areas |
| Policy Categories | Productive Natural Resources | Productive Natural Resources | Productive Natural Resources |
| Policy Sub-categories | Forestry | Fisheries | Agriculture |
| Indicators | Growing Stock | Marine Tropic Index, Trawling Intensity | Irrigation Stress, Agricultural Subsidies, Intensive Cropland, Burnt Land Area, Pesticide Regulation |
| Policy Categories | Climate Change | | |
| Indicators | Emissions per capita, Emissions per electricity generated, Industrial carbon intensity | | |

*Source:* EPI 2012 Full Report, available at www.epi.yale.edu.

### Box 6   Sustainable Development

Sustainable Development concerns pattern of resource use that aims at meeting human needs while preserving the environment. Essentially, this involves that the needs should be met not only in the present, but also for the generations to come. The most oft-quoted definition of sustainable development coined by Brundtland Commission is development that 'meets the needs of the present without compromising the ability of future generations to meet their own needs'.

The concept of 'sustainable development' had established a link between environmental protection and development at large. As early as in the 1970s sustainability was employed to describe an economy 'in equilibrium with basic ecological support systems'.

**TABLE 3** Environmental Performance Index, 2012

| Strongest Performers | Score | Strong Performers | Score | Modest Performers | Score | Weak Performers | Score |
|---|---|---|---|---|---|---|---|
| Switzerland | 76.69 | Germany | 66.91 | Georgia | 56.84 | Togo | 48.66 |
| Latvia | 70.37 | Slovakia | 66.62 | Australia | 56.61 | Algeria | 48.56 |
| Norway | 69.92 | Iceland | 66.28 | United States of America | 56.59 | Malta | 48.51 |
| Luxembourg | 69.20 | New Zealand | 66.05 | Cuba | 56.48 | Romania | 48.34 |
| Costa Rica | 69.03 | Albania | 65.85 | Argentina | 56.48 | Mozambique | 47.82 |
| France | 69.00 | Netherlands | 65.65 | Singapore | 56.36 | Angola | 47.57 |
| Austria | 68.92 | Lithuania | 65.50 | Bulgaria | 56.28 | Ghana | 47.50 |
| Italy | 68.90 | Czech Republic | 64.79 | Estonia | 56.09 | Dem. Rep. Congo | 47.49 |
| United Kingdom | 68.82 | Finland | 64.44 | Sri Lanka | 55.72 | Armenia | 47.48 |
| Sweden | 68.82 | Croatia | 64.16 | Venezuela | 55.62 | Lebanon | 47.35 |
| | | Denmark | 63.61 | Zambia | 55.56 | Congo | 47.18 |
| | | Poland | 63.47 | Chile | 55.34 | Trinidad and Tobago | 47.04 |
| | | Japan | 63.36 | Cambodia | 55.29 | Macedonia | 46.96 |
| Weakest Performers | Score | Belgium | 63.02 | Egypt | 55.18 | Senegal | 46.73 |
| Tajikistan | 38.78 | Malaysia | 62.51 | Israel | 54.64 | Tunisia | 46.66 |
| Eritrea | 38.39 | Brunei Darussalam | 62.49 | Bolivia | 54.57 | Qatar | 46.59 |
| Libyan Arab Jamahiriya | 37.68 | Colombia | 62.33 | Jamaica | 54.36 | Kyrgyzstan | 46.33 |

| Country | Value | Country | Value | Country | Value | Country | Value |
|---|---|---|---|---|---|---|---|
| Bosnia and Herzegovina | 36.76 | Slovenia | 62.25 | Tanzania | 54.26 | Ukraine | 46.31 |
| India | 36.23 | Taiwan | 62.23 | Belarus | 53.88 | Serbia | 46.14 |
| Kuwait | 35.54 | Brazil | 60.90 | Botswana | 53.74 | Sudan | 46.00 |
| Yemen | 35.49 | Ecuador | 60.55 | Côte d'Ivoire | 53.55 | Morocco | 45.76 |
| South Africa | 34.55 | Spain | 60.31 | Zimbabwe | 52.76 | Russia | 45.43 |
| Kazakhstan | 32.94 | Greece | 60.04 | Myanmar | 52.72 | Mongolia | 45.37 |
| Uzbekistan | 32.24 | Thailand | 59.98 | Ethiopia | 52.71 | Moldova | 45.21 |
| Turkmenistan | 31.75 | Nicaragua | 59.23 | Honduras | 52.54 | Turkey | 44.80 |
| Iraq | 25.00 | Ireland | 58.69 | Dominican Republic | 52.44 | Oman | 44.00 |
| | | Canada | 58.41 | Paraguay | 52.40 | Azerbaijan | 43.11 |
| | | Nepal | 57.97 | Indonesia | 52.29 | Cameroon | 42.97 |
| | | Panama | 57.94 | El Salvador | 52.08 | Syria | 42.75 |
| | | Gabon | 57.91 | Guatemala | 51.88 | Iran | 42.73 |
| | | Portugal | 57.64 | UAE | 50.91 | Bangladesh | 42.55 |
| | | Philippines | 57.40 | Namibia | 50.68 | China | 42.24 |
| | | South Korea | 57.20 | Viet Nam | 50.64 | Jordan | 42.16 |
| | | Cyprus | 57.15 | Benin | 50.38 | Haiti | 41.15 |
| | | Hungary | 57.12 | Peru | 50.29 | Nigeria | 40.14 |
| | | Uruguay | 57.06 | Saudi Arabia | 49.97 | Pakistan | 39.56 |
| | | | | Kenya | 49.28 | | |
| | | | | Mexico | 49.11 | | |

*Source:* Available at http://epi.yale.edu.

# 2

# International Trade and Environmental Damage

There are several dimensions to international trade affecting the environment—adverse as well as advantageous. These dimensions make it difficult to provide any straightforward answer to the apparently simple question of trade raising pollution. First, one must distinguish whether it is the country-specific environmental effects of increased trade (and hence national pollution levels) or global effects of such trade that is under consideration. For example, most of the environmental analyses of large economy-wide events—such as trade liberalization—focus on global pollutants such as carbon dioxide emissions and changes in its levels. There are also sector-specific country studies that focus on national pollution. Of course, as exemplified in the previous chapter, on many occasions it is diffi-cult to segregate country-specific and global pollution effects of a particular economic activity. But even in the instances where environmental damages are con-fined to certain geographical or national boundaries, the answer to the question posed earlier—whether increased trade raises national pollution levels—depends largely on whether pollution emission takes place while the good is being produced or while it is being consumed. Moreover, in either case, effects on the national environments of trading nations are com-pletely asymmetric. A country exporting a dirty good will experience greater environmental damage in the case of production pollution whereas the importing country will experience a less polluted environment when trade between them expands. That is, the answer to the question posed depends also on the pattern of comparative advantage of nations.

The second dimension involves normative and policy issues. It is undeniable that when nations trade according to their *genuine* comparative advantage signalled correctly through the costs and prices, there will be substantial gains that arise through exchange and production specialization. Thus, if trade affects the local environment adversely, there will be a trade-off between gains from trade and ensuing environmental degradation. The policy issue that crops up then is: *should free trade be restricted to protect national environments?*

The third dimension is that environmental damages caused by polluting production activities may also have adverse impacts on other spheres of the production economy. In that case, the cost of pollution, apart from the direct loss of utility suffered by the society, makes itself felt as a loss of productivity in other sectors of production. The implication of international trade in such instances is altogether different from that when such *externalities* are absent and there are only the direct utility losses from environmental degradation.

This chapter discusses the issues which arise when environmental damage caused by economic activities are essentially localized and confined to national boundaries. Trans-boundary or global pollution issues will be discussed in later chapters. Moreover, we will confine ourselves here to the static effects of increased trade on the national environment. The long-run effect of trade through growth will be discussed in Chapter 3.

# Scale, Composition, and Technique Effects

Free trade affects the environment in three ways. Suppose an economy produces goods that can be ranked according to their pollution emission or pollution intensity per unit of output produced. Such goods are dirtier if they emit more pollution relative to other goods. As trade opens up, the country specializes in goods in which it has a comparative advantage, and if these goods are dirtier, the overall pollution should increase. If initially, all resources were fully employed, expansion of production of dirtier goods requires contraction of other goods that are by assumption relatively cleaner, and release of resources from such production. Free trade in that case changes the composition of aggregate output towards relatively dirtier goods if the country has comparative advantage in those goods. This is the *composition effect* of free trade whereby overall national pollution may rise. But, if initially resources were not fully employed, free trade will increase scale of production of dirtier goods without requiring a contraction of production elsewhere. National pollution rises once again through this *scale effect*. In fact, scale effect will arise even when resources are fully employed as will be illustrated in the later sections.

Finally, free trade may induce producers to adopt cleaner production techniques by altering factor prices and the relative cost of emission. This *technique effect* lowers national pollution. Overall, composition and scale effects dominate the technique effect so that free trade raises the pollution level in the country having comparative advantage in dirtier goods and, consequently, exporting these goods. The same logic implies that through similar composition, scale, and technique effects, the national pollution level in the countries importing the dirtier goods should fall. The appendix provides a simple algebra to understand these three effects of trade on the national pollution level.

Following Copeland and Taylor (2003), these three effects are illustrated in Figure 1. Consider a small open economy that faces a given set of world prices of the two goods that it produces. Good X is the dirty good that pollutes the environment when it is produced and good Y is the clean good. The bowed-out curve *MN* represents the production possibility frontier (PPF)— the different combination of the dirty and clean goods that can be produced, exhausting all the resources of

34

the economy. The downward slope of the PPF reflects that expansion of the production of one good can be realized only when the production of the other good is lowered and, thus, resources are released from that sector. The bowed-out shape of the PPF, on the other hand, reflects that the rate at which, say, production of good Y must fall for realization of one unit of expansion of good X increases with successive expansion of production. That is, the opportunity cost of producing the dirty good rises with its production. The pre-trade production is organized at point A where the pre-trade price line—absolute slope of which reflects the price of the dirty good X relative to that of clean good Y— is tangent to the PPF. The ray emanating from the origin through this point gives us the pre-trade production ratio $Y/X$. If this economy has a comparative advantage in the dirty good X, the post-trade relative price of good X that it will face will be higher as shown by the steeper broken line through pre-trade production point A. The post-trade production adjusts to point C with the country specializing (incompletely though) in the production of the dirty good X. The composition of production now changes towards the dirty good as the production ratio falls to $Y'/X'$.

Pollution, thus, rises as shown in the lower panel of Figure 1. The ray through the origin reflects the relation between total pollution denoted by $Z$ and output of the dirty good X, where $e$ denotes the per unit emission.

This increase in pollution can be broken down into two components. First, increase in pollution from $Z_0$ to $Z_1$ corresponding to the increase in production of

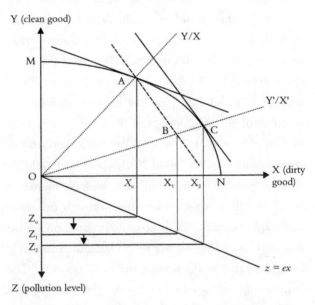

**FIGURE 1**    Scale and Composition Effect of Free Trade

good X from $X_o$ to $X_1$ units. This is the composition effect because this expansion in production of good X corresponds to the movement from point $A$ to point $B$ along the same price line and, hence, captures the change in composition of the *same* aggregate value of production. The increase in pollution emission from $Z_1$ to $Z_2$, on the other hand, reflects the scale effect. The increase in production of the dirty good that causes this part of the increase in total pollution corresponds to the movement from $B$ to $C$ along the same ray, reflecting an increase in the scale of production of both goods (and commensurate increase in the value of aggregate production as indicated by the higher parallel price line on which point $C$ lies) without any change in composition of output.

On top of these composition and scale effects, a *technique effect* arises if one considers the environment as an input to the production process of dirty good X. For instance, suppose producers of good X are forced to internalize the social cost of environmental degradation through a pollution tax. The pollution tax rate is imposed in a way to make tax payments exactly equal to the divergence between marginal social cost and marginal private cost of producing the dirty good.

Thus, the pollution tax rate is the price of environmental input. Now, with opening up of trade and arbitrage, as the relative price of the dirty good rises, the price of environmental input rises relative to other inputs. This is because the dirty good being relatively intensive in the use of the environmental input, the relative demand for such input rises and thereby causes its price to rise. This increased relative price of the environmental input induces all producers to choose a lower pollution-intensive production technique. Therefore, by the technique effect, gross pollution should decline.

However, on the whole, we can expect the composition and scale effects to be larger, so that trade liberalization raises the overall national pollution level in the country exporting the dirty good, when production process degrades the environment. The flip-side is that overall national pollution should decline in the country importing the dirty good.

On the other hand, when consumption of a good, rather than its production, degrades the environment, international trade shifts the pollution load to the country importing the dirty good. That is, pollution is exported to the consuming country. A similar decomposition of pollution generated in the country exporting the dirty good is illustrated in Figure 2. The pre-trade and post-trade consumption points are denoted by A and C, respectively. The increased consumption from X units to X" units increases pollution, which is again the sum of the composition and scale effects. The composition effect is the movement from consumption point A to consumption point B along the same aggregate value of consumption line, whereby only the ratio in which the dirty and clean goods are consumed changes. Note that trade lowers the consumption of the dirty good to X' and thus pollution in the exporting country declines. This composition effect is, in fact, the substitution effect—consumers change their consumption ratio as the relative price of the dirty good rises after trade expands. The scale effect, on the other hand, is represented by the movement from consumption point B to consumption point C, and is analogous to the *income* effect—the change in the consumption of goods when incomes of consumers change. The consumption of the dirty good now rises (proportionate to the consumption of the clean good along the same consumption ray), and with it rises the pollution level. But, as long as tastes are homothetic, which is the underlying assumption of Figure 2, this scale (or income) effect will be smaller in magnitude than the composition effect. Hence, overall pollution declines in the exporting country.

Summing up, the answer to the question—how does free trade affect national pollution levels—depends on, first, whether it is a case of production pollution or consumption pollution; and second, the pattern of trade. Moreover, the direction in which international trade shifts the pollution load also depends on these

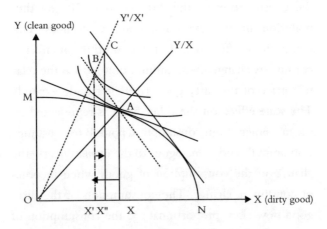

**FIGURE 2**   Consumption Pollution in the Exporting Country

two aspects. In particular, in the case of production pollution, international trade shifts the pollution load from the country importing dirty goods to the country exporting them. In the case of consumption pollution, the reverse holds true.

## Trade-off between Gains from Trade and Environmental Degradation

The important policy issue that crops up from the earlier discussion is that if increased trade degrades the environment, and thereby inflicts social losses, should international trade be restricted or prohibited? The answer is unambiguously negative for several reasons. First, a well-known result in international trade theory since the time of David Ricardo is that if countries trade according to their comparative advantages, real income gains from such trade will be realized for all trading nations. Of course, real incomes gains are realized not for all agents in the economy, but, overall, gainers gain more than the losers lose. Thus, when produced goods degrade the environment and inflict social losses, these are to be weighed against the real income gains from opening up of trade.

41

Second, environmental degradation through pollution emission is a typical case of negative externality—production or consumption as the case may be—that requires a domestic policy intervention rather than trade intervention. This result is well established in international trade literature by Harry Johnson and Jagdish Bhagwati, in their pioneering works. Free trade with environmental taxes or regulations is the first best policy. Negative externality creates divergence between private and social costs as the relevant agents do not internalize the costs they inflict upon others. In case of production pollution, the producers of the dirty good overproduce the good. This requires production taxes or regulations as the optimal corrective policy.

To illustrate, consider Figure 3 which depicts a perfectly competitive market for an industrial good. The marginal cost (MC) of production rises with the output level. Competition forces producers to charge a price equal to the MC of production. Thus, given the downward sloping domestic demand curve, the unregulated competitive industry produces level $Q$ of output under autarchy (or no trade situation) and charges the price $Ob$ corresponding to the intersection point $c$ between the $D$ and $MC$ curves. Suppose industrial wastes are dumped into an adjacent water body, which is a source of drinking water for the local inhabitants. The water pollution causes health hazards for these people and raises their health expenditures or medical bills for curing the ailment. But being unregulated, the producers do not internalize this social cost measured by the additional health expenditures that they inflict upon the local inhabitants. The social

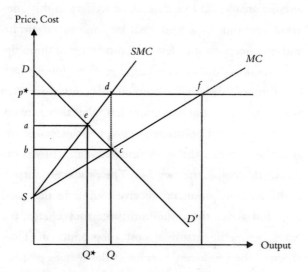

**FIGURE 3** Negative Production Externality, Over-production, and Output Tax

marginal cost (SMC) of producing the industrial good is thus larger than the (private) MC. Moreover, greater is the output level, larger is this divergence.

A social planner, taking into account this externality in production of this industrial good, would have charged a higher price $Oa$ (equal to the SMC of production) and produce a lower output level $Q^*$. An unregulated private economy, thus, overproduces. The consequent loss in social welfare equals the triangular area '$edc$'. Note that social welfare in this one-good economy is a sum total of consumers' surplus and producers' surplus less the costs inflicted upon the local residents due to consumption of polluted water. Consumers' surplus is the amount that consumers were willing to pay at the maximum less what they actually pay. At the social optimum output $Q^*$, this equals the area $Dae$, whereas at the unregulated competitive output Q, this equals the area $Dbc$. The producers' surplus is the amount producers receive by selling the good over and above the minimum price they charge, the latter being the marginal cost of production. Thus, whereas the producers' surplus at the social optimum equals the area $aeS$, at the unregulated competitive output it equals the area $bcS$. Thus, consumers' and producers' surplus together is higher at the competitive output than at the social optimum: $ScD > SeD$. The net gain is the triangular area *gce*. But, unregulated competitive production inflicts a cost on the local inhabitants, which is measured by the area *egcd*. Thus, the gain in consumers' and producers' surplus at output level $Q$ is to be weighed against the additional loss on the part of the local inhabitants due to drinking of polluted water. Hence, unregulated competitive economy leads to a net loss in social welfare by the area *edc*.

This distortion, or the loss of social welfare, at the unregulated competitive equilibrium, can be corrected through, among other instruments, an output tax that varies with the output level at the rate that is just enough to raise the marginal cost of production of the private producers (now inclusive of the tax) to the level of the social marginal cost. Thus, under this production or output tax, the private producers perceive the *SMC* curve as their (tax inclusive) marginal cost. Consequently, the regulated industry output exactly equals the socially optimum output $Q^*$. The market price is $Oa$, what the social planner would have charged. But, the producers now receive a lower price net of taxes, $Op'$. The government collects a tax revenue to the amount as indicated by the area *aegp'*. Pigou (1912) was the first to point out that the government should tax those who inflict external costs and subsidize those whose acts generate positive externalities for the society. This policy of tax or subsidy to correct externalities is known as Pigouvian policy.

Note that the optimal tax policy achieves two things. First, it forces the producers to *fully* internalize the external costs that they inflict on the local inhabitants, and second, in the process, corrects for the overproduction of the good that would occur at the unregulated equilibrium. Similar argument shows that in case of consumption pollution (and negative consumption externality), the optimum policy calls for a (domestic) consumption tax. Policy instruments other than production tax (in case of production pollution) or consumption tax (in case of consumption pollution) do not work to the extent required to correct the existing distortion. This follows from the general rule for optimal intervention set out by Harry G. Johnson (1965) in the context of externalities and other sources of distortions. The policy intervention, which by itself creates a distortion in the system and is thus aimed to counter an existing distortion, should be at the exact sphere of economic activity where the distortion exists and the magnitude of the policy intervention (or the rate of tax) must be just enough to offset the existing distortion, neither more nor less. By this rule, if a consumption tax was imposed in the above example of production pollution, it would not have been effective as it would fail to force the producers to internalize the external costs.

There are, of course, other ways to correct this distortion such as assigning property rights for the water body to any of the contesting agent groups. The social optimum, then, can be arrived at through bargaining amongst the economic agents. This purely market solution was first pointed out by Ronald Coase, which works, however, under certain limiting assumptions regarding size of the contesting agents and complexities of the externality problem (see Box 7).

But, as it follows from the above mentioned general rule for optimal intervention, restricting trade cannot be an optimal policy. A similar point has been raised by Bhagwati and Srinivasan (1996). Trade restriction does not force the producers to internalize the externality though it does restrict production. At the same time, it distorts the domestic prices that the producers receive and consumers pay for the traded goods. Thus, the social welfare loss may, in fact, be larger when trade is restricted. This can be explained as follows. Suppose the dirty good is being exported by this economy, and the local government restricts exports through an export tax. But an export tax is essentially a combination of production tax and consumption subsidy. The latter effect follows from the fact that an export tax lowers the domestic price of the good. Thus, an export tax introduces a larger distortion in the system than is required to offset the existing externality problem.

Furthermore, recalling Figure 3, suppose the world price of this good (for this small open economy, say) is $Op^*$, with domestic production of the unregulated economy being $p^*h$ and exports being $hf$. Had the economy been regulated through a production tax, exports would have been smaller at the socially optimum $hd$ level, with $p^*dcp$ going to the government exchequer. Now, if only export is banned or completely prohibited, instead of trade being allowed with a production tax, the policy intervention would have been clearly suboptimal, since we return to the case we started with: producers overproduce (for the domestic economy since trade is prohibited) and inflict a social loss to the amount of the area *edc*. But if exports were allowed with producers paying a production tax, the economy would have a net gain, measured by the triangular area *edh*. Thus, production pollution (and for similar reasons, consumption pollution) never calls for prohibiting or restricting trade. This is often misunderstood and misperceived among environmentalists.

## International Trade and Spatial Separation

An interesting and beneficial role of international trade may arise when it spatially separates out dirty and clean industries across countries, and thereby lowers aggregate pollution. This beneficial role of international trade through the spatial separation of economic activities is particularly important when dirty goods production generates negative externalities for the clean industries.

In the discussion so far, the environmental damage caused by polluting production activities has a direct negative effect on the welfare of the population. International trade and the consequent specialization

## Box 7  Assigning Property Rights as an Alternative Solution

Ronald Coase (1960) argued that assigning property rights for the water body is an alternative market-based solution for the negative externality in the above example. To see how his argument goes through, regardless of whether the property right is assigned to the polluter or the polluted, suppose local inhabitants get the property right of the water body. Then, provided that the legal system works efficiently, local inhabitants can force the producers to compensate them for dumping industrial waste in the water body and, thereby, causing health hazards. The producers internalize this compensation cost and cut back production to the socially optimum level. If instead, the property right is assigned to the producers, the local inhabitants can bribe them for not dumping industrial waste in the water body. The amount of bribe would be to the extent of the losses they suffer from water pollution. Now the producers internalize the social cost of dumping waste and produce up to the socially optimum level because overproduction means corresponding bribe foregone. Thus, there is now an opportunity cost of overproduction, which makes their private cost calculations exactly the same as the social marginal cost.

There are a few caveats to this argument known as the Coase theorem. First, there can be significantly positive transaction costs involved in this kind of bargaining to arrive at the social optimum. Second, if the parties involved are too many, implementing this mechanism becomes almost infeasible. For example, when hundreds of jute mills and industrial units on the West Bank of the Ganges near Kolkata dump waste in the river water and millions of people use the Ganges as source of their drinking water and fishing, the major problem is to whom the property right should be assigned. Moreover, for such a large number of people involved, both polluter and victims, it is almost impossible to get together and reach an agreement.

only serve to reinforce and magnify this loss of welfare. But environmental degradation caused by polluting production activities may also impact adversely other spheres of the production economy. In that case, the cost of pollution, apart from the direct loss of utility suffered by the society, makes itself felt as a loss of productivity in other sectors of production. An interesting aspect of such a cross effect is that international trade, unlike in the case discussed above, may reduce the ill effects of pollution rather than magnify them. There are potential gains from trade on this count for the world economy that the trading partners can share.

Copeland and Taylor (1999) were the first to point out this beneficial aspect of international trade. Consider the case where industrial production emits industrial ashes into the air, which is transported by the wind and then deposited on the earth's surface through rain. Such 'wet' deposition of industrial ashes erode soil fertility and thus raise the cost of agricultural production as the farmers have to increase the use of fertilizers to maintain the same yield per acre as before. In a no-trade situation, the economy must produce both the industrial goods and food grains to meet domestic demand. Consequently, the economy bears not only the direct loss of utility from environmental degradation (air pollution in this example) but also the loss of agricultural productivity. But international trade allows the economy to meet its demand for either industrial goods or food grains entirely through imports instead of domestic production. A social planner can, thus, improve social welfare through a spatial separation of industrial and agricultural activities that trade allows, by devoting all resources only to the production of, say, industrial goods and importing all the requirement of food grains. Of course, this might be in conflict with other national interests such as food security, but from the social welfare perspective this is a desired option, provided of course such a pattern of complete specialization and consequently spatial separation of economic activities is consistent with the economy's comparative advantage. Note, that both under constant and decreasing marginal cost conditions, complete specialization would be a market outcome as well. The typical example is the production technologies that require the use of inputs in a fixed ratio in both industrial and agricultural production. This makes the marginal costs of production independent of the level of output. Cross country price difference that triggers arbitrage and trading of commodities thus persist even though each country expands the production of the commodity in which it has a comparative advantage. The scope of arbitrage thus induces the countries to expand production successively till resources shifted from other lines of production are exhausted and the countries are completely specialized in their respective comparative advantage goods.

In sum, the negative impact of industry on productivity in agriculture can be avoided through international trade when market conditions allow spatial separation of these activities. As Copeland and Taylor (1999) demonstrate, this raises all-round productivity and both trading partners benefit.

## International Trade and Pollution: Empirical Estimates

Most empirical studies estimating the pollution effect of trade liberalization focus on the *composition* effect. That is, whether trade liberalization shifts the composition of aggregate output towards dirty industrial production. However, the definition and measure of dirty industries vary from one study to the other. Lucas Wheeler, and Hettige (1992), for example, ranked industries on the basis of aggregate toxic releases per unit of output. By this criterion, they identified metals, cement, pulp and paper, and chemicals as the dirtiest industries. Analysing the toxic intensity of manufacturing in 80 countries between 1960 and 1988, Lucas et al. found that the dirty (toxic-intensive) industries grew faster in the relatively closed, fast growing developing countries, rather than in the countries that were most open to trade. Regional work on Latin America has generated similar results (Birdsall and Wheeler 1993). On the other hand, Rock (1996) found that toxic pollution loads per dollar of gross domestic product (GDP) for a country as a whole was positively correlated with measures of openness to trade during 1973–85. That is, the more open the trade policy, the greater is the pollution intensity.

The most comprehensive study of estimating the three static effects of trade liberalization was done by Antweiler, Copeland, and Taylor (2001). They examined the relative contribution of each of the aforementioned effects of openness to international trade in terms of sulfur dioxide $(SO_2)$ concentrations. They concluded that *freer trade is good for the environment.* They observed very little change in $SO_2$ emissions from changes in the composition of national output. On the other hand, estimates of trade-induced technology and scale effects imply a net reduction in pollution. The authors estimate that for every 1 per cent increase in national income resulting from trade liberalization, there is a 0.8 to 0.9 per cent reduction in concentrations of $SO_2$. Estimations by Frankel and Rose (2005), however, produced mixed results. They estimated the effects of openness on particulate matter, $SO_2$, nitrogen dioxide ($NO_2$), carbon dioxide ($CO_2$), deforestation, and access to clean water. The results showed that for air pollution measures ($SO_2$, $NO_2$, and particulate matter), openness reduces pollution. Trade openness also has beneficial, though marginal, effects on energy depletion, and clean water access. But, trade openness raises the $CO_2$ emissions, which is a global pollutant.

Overall, there seem to be beneficial effects of trade openness on national pollution levels, as measured by local pollutants. However, most of these benefits accrue through the growth effect of trade openness as well, as shall be discussed in the next chapter that growth is mostly beneficial for environment.

Chattopadhyay (2005) finds that the pollution content of India's trade basket had increased during 1985–2000, the period during which the country-brought about major economic reforms including exchange rate and trade liberalization. Thus, increased trade during this period seems to have led India to specialize more in dirtier goods, indicating the adverse *composition* effect. The study by Gamper–Rabindran and Jha (2004) also shows that there has been a moderate increase in air and water pollution-intensive exports in the post-liberalization period compared to pre-liberalization.

# Appendix

The following break-down of total pollution effect is drawn from Copeland and Taylor (2003). Let $e = Z/x$ denote emissions per unit of output ($X$), where $Z$ is the total pollution emission.

Let the value of output at a given level of world prices be the measure of the economy's scale, $S$:

$$S = pX + Y$$

where $p$ denotes the relative world price of good $X$ (in terms of good $Y$), or the terms of trade.

For a small country, the terms of trade do not change, and thus we normalize it to unity. Hence, the scale of output is simply the sum of physical units of the two outputs. Let $\beta = X/S$, which is, in fact, the share of the dirty good production in aggregate production. Thus, this variable captures the 'composition' effect.

Hence pollution emissions, $Z$, depend on the emissions intensity of production, $e$, the share of the dirty good industry in the economy, $\beta$, and the scale of the economy, $S$:

$$Z = eX = e\beta S$$

Taking logarithm and totally differentiating we obtain the decomposition of the change in pollution emission:

$$\hat{Z} = \hat{S} + \hat{\beta} + \hat{e}$$

where the hat over a variable denotes its proportional change, for example, $\hat{Z} = \dfrac{dZ}{Z}$. The first term is the scale effect. It measures the increase in pollution that would be generated if the economy were simply scaled up, holding constant the aggregate value of production and production techniques. The second term is the *composition* effect as captured by the change in the share of the dirty good in aggregate production. The third term is the *technique* effect. *Ceteris paribus*, a reduction in the emissions intensity will reduce pollution.

# 3

# Trade, Growth, and Environmental Degradation

Many trade theorists have argued that trade and the resultant growth may be good for the environment. If environmental quality is a normal good, increases in income brought about by trade or growth will increase both the demand for environmental quality and the ability of governments to afford costly investments in environmental protection. Hence, growth due to increased trade should lower aggregate pollution levels in trading nations.

The growth effect of trade liberalization on the environment is, at best, an indirect relationship: trade augments income growth, and income growth affects pollution levels. This chapter discusses this indirect growth effect of international trade. It begins with a brief review of the trade–growth relationship, followed by the growth–pollution relationship.

## Trade and Growth

Trade liberalization affects economic growth in more than one way. First of all, there is the characterization of trade as an engine of growth by Sir Dennis Robertson. Similar ideas can be traced back to writings of the classical economists. For example, according to Adam Smith, international trade provides a vent for surplus productive capacities by changing the domestic terms of trade between industry and agriculture. Malthus, on the other hand, perceived the contribution of trade in the growth process to be one of offsetting diminishing returns in agriculture and increasing the labour supply by affecting the work–leisure choice. International trade expands the consumption set by making available foreign goods and therefore encourages people to increase their work effort at any given wage rate.

The second set of arguments, which are neo-classical in tradition, evolve around the gains from trade and income redistribution effects. As international trade raises the real income of trading nations, it allows for a higher rate of savings, capital formation, and therefore output growth. On the other hand, the redistribution effect of trade alters the rate of output growth if people have different marginal propensities to save. For example, if trade lowers the money wage and raises the rate of return to capital, there will be an overall increase in savings propensity since capitalists usually have a higher marginal propensity to save than the wage earners. Consequently there will be higher rates of capital accumulation and growth. Of course, if trade redistributes incomes in a different way, growth may be impeded. An interesting implication of this redistributive effect of trade on growth deserves attention. Consider the opening up of trade between two countries: United States and India. Suppose India has a comparative advantage in relatively labour-intensive cotton textiles, whereas the United States has a comparative advantage in relatively capital-intensive personal computers. That is, the relative pre-trade price of cotton textiles is lower in India compared to that in the United States. Conversely, the relative pre-trade price of computers is lower in the United States compared to that of India. These comparative advantages may be the outcomes of the capital abundance of the

61

United States and the labour abundance of India. As trade opens up, arbitrage and consequent movement of goods—computers being exported by the United States to India, and cotton textiles being exported by India to the United States—leads to the equalization of relative prices across these two countries. Thus, after trade, the relative price of cotton textiles rises in India and the same declines in the United States. The well-known Stolper–Samuelson theorem states that an increase in the relative price of the labour-intensive good raises the return to labour relative to the return to capital (see Box 8). Hence, the asymmetric price movement in the two countries after trade should mean that the redistributive effects of opening up of trade in India and the United States would be in the opposite direction. Hence, growth experiences of these two countries should be different as well, *ceteris paribus*. Similar asymmetric redistributive effects of trade and subsequent growth implications may arise for simultaneous trade liberalization by countries trading with each other.

Countries' experiences regarding trade and its effects on growth are mixed. Frankel and Romer (1999) find that the trade openness index is strongly related to

## Box 8    Stolper–Samuelson Theorem

Stolper and Samuelson (1941: 51–68) established that when a country imposes a tariff on its imports, the real wage will increase and real return to capital will fall as a consequence, if imports are relatively labour-intensive and exports are relatively capital-intensive. Taking their argument to trade liberalization through a tariff cut, workers should then lose (gain) and capitalists gain (lose) when imports are relatively labour- (capital-) intensive. The logic behind this interesting result is simple. A tariff cut lowers the price of imports in the liberalizing country and thus raises import volume. Competition from imports displaces local production of the import competing good and the resources thus released move into the export sector to expand production there. But if the imports (import-competing good, more precisely) are relatively labour-intensive then the contracting import-competing sector will release more labour and less capital than can be absorbed in the expanding capital-intensive export sector. Thus, emerging excess supply of labour and excess demand for capital as the economy adjusts its composition of aggregate output will lower wage and raise the rate of return to capital. What is more, the wage will fall more than proportionate to the fall in the import price. Hence, the real wage falls as well.

long-term growth, though there is no reverse causation from growth to trade. Others, however, are skeptical about the positive impact of trade openness on growth. For example, Rodriguez and Rodrik (1999) show that the robustness of the correlation between the openness measure and growth *declines* as other variables (such as institutions like growth of property rights) are added to the analysis. In an interesting study, on the other hand, Dollar and Kraay (2001) found that in the 1990s, the globalizing developing countries were catching up with rich countries, whereas the relatively closed ones continued to lag further behind. The post-1980 globalized group of countries had a particularly large increase in trade of 104 per cent compared to 71 per cent for the rich countries, and had also cut their import tariffs by almost 34 points. These recent globalizing economies have experienced accelerated growth rates, much higher than what the relatively closed ones have achieved.

More recent refinements in the empirical estimates of the trade and growth relationship reveal that it is not so much a matter of how much a country exports but what it exports. Rodrik (2006), for example, observes that for China, it is not the volume of export or specialization according to comparative advantage in labour-intensive exports but her export of highly sophisticated product that has been the main driver of its rapid growth during the 1990s and thereafter. Significant output growth for many East Asian and Latin American countries can also be largely explained by growth in high and medium technology exports by these countries (Aditya and Acharyya 2011). Table 4 reports the high correlation between GDP and high technology exports for selected countries in these regions.

**TABLE 4**  High Technology Exports and GDP in 2002

| Countries | Correlation Coefficient |
|---|---|
| *Asia* | |
| China | 0.99 |
| Indonesia | 0.67 |
| Korea | 0.87 |
| Singapore | 0.99 |
| Thailand | 0.9 |
| *Latin America* | |
| Argentina | 0.75 |
| Brazil | 0.82 |
| Chile | 0.86 |
| Mexico | 0.69 |

*Source:* Author's compilation based on *World Development Indicator 2005.*

These observations are somewhat consistent with the New Growth Theories that identify sources of growth as either increasing product variety or quality (Grossman and Helpman 1991). Hausmann et al. (2007), on the other hand, found that a measure of productivity associated with a country's export basket has a significant positive impact on economic growth.

## Growth and the Environment

Like trade liberalization, income growth also has three effects on the magnitude of pollution emissions. Greater economic activity raises the demand for all inputs, including environment as free input, and hence increases emissions. This is the *scale effect*. On the other hand, if people increase their demand for a clean environment as their incomes rise, they will then tolerate higher levels of pollution only if the effluent charge is higher. Since higher effluent charges encourage firms to shift toward cleaner production processes, this *technique effect* tends to reduce emissions. On top of this, if income growth shifts preferences toward cleaner goods, that is, if clean goods are relatively income elastic, then the share of pollution–intensive goods in output will fall. This *composition effect*, therefore, tends to decrease emissions. Note that this composition effect of growth is demand-driven rather than production-driven as in the case of the short-run effect of trade liberalization discussed in the earlier chapter.

As Copeland and Taylor (1994) demonstrated, growth and pollution may have an altogether different relationship between them under free trade than under autarchy (no trade). If marginal environmental damage is proportional to income growth, the *scale* and *technique* effects of growth cancel each other out under autarchy. However, under free trade, growth in the North raises both Northern and Southern pollution, whereas growth in the South lowers both Northern and Southern pollution.

The source of economic growth is also important in determining the income growth and the pollution level of the growing country. To illustrate, let us consider our two-commodity two-factor framework of a small open economy discussed in the Chapter 2. Suppose, for any given factor price ratio, the dirty good X uses more capital than labour relative to the use of these factors by the production process of the clean good. If growth occurs via the accumulation of physical capital, by the well-known Rybczynski theorem (see Box 9), the production of the dirty good expands whereas that of the clean good declines. This *composition* effect of growth, thus, raises pollution levels. That is, income and pollution are positively (and monotonically) related. When the labour force grows as well, though is less than proportionate to the rate of capital accumulation, once again the composition of output shifts towards the dirty good. But, now there may be a scale effect, in addition to the composition effect, because the production of the clean good Y may expand as well along with a larger expansion of the dirty good. This difference in the two cases can be explained as follows. In the case of a *ceteris paribus* accumulation in capital, if initially all workers were productively engaged the expansion of dirty good production would require and be constrained by the decline in the production of the clean good Y. This is because, without any growth in the labour force, additional labour required to sustain the expansion of the capital-intensive dirty good would be available (without any immigration of workers from abroad) only through the reduction of production elsewhere, and the consequent release of labour from that contracting sector. However, in the process, relatively capital-intensive dirty good production expands more than proportionately to the growth of capital because the contracting sector also releases capital along with labour. However, when the labour force also grows (though less than proportionately to the growth in capital), to expand the production of the capital-intensive dirty good, the production of the other good(s) may not need to decline to release labour. That would still be a necessity only if the labour force grows too little compared to the growth of capital. Thus, depending on the relative growth in factor endowments, the production of the clean good in our example may rise or fall. However, even when it rises, the expansion would be less than proportionate to the growth in the labour force. Hence, like the previous case, the composition of output shifts towards the dirty good's production.

On the other hand, income and pollution will have a monotonic *negative* relationship when only labour force grows, or when labour force grows relative to the growth of capital. This is because, by the Rybczynski theorem, the composition of output will shift towards the production of the clean good. Hence, growth will lower pollution.

Thus, we can expect different income and pollution paths for different (internal) sources of growth. Therefore, it would be misleading to draw an analogy between the damaging effects of economic development and those of liberalized trade. But, in any case, the theory suggests a stable monotonic relation between pollution, income, and factor endowments.

---

### Box 9   Rybczynski Theorem

In a two-commodity, two-factor world, Rybczynski (1955) demonstrated that given the set of commodity prices, a 10 per cent (say) growth in physical capital raises the production of the capital-intensive good by more than 10 per cent and *lowers* the production of the other labour-intensive good. Generalizing, if capital grows more than proportionate to the labour force growth, the increase in the production of the capital-intensive good would be more than the growth in capital, and the increase in the production of the other good (if at all) would be the least. This is also known as the output magnification effect, in the sense that output changes are magnification of the changes in factor endowments. Hence, supply of the capital-intensive good, relative to that of the labour-intensive good, rises.

---

However, as Copeland and Taylor (2003) emphasize, at the cross-country level, we can still observe a non-monotonic relation between income growth and pollution because not all countries grow exactly in the same way. Empirical estimates of such a possibility are reported below.

## Empirical Estimates: Environmental Kuznets Curve

Empirical estimates reveal that the growth–emission relationship is non-monotonic. The pioneering empirical work in this regard was by Grossman and Krueger (1993). Using a panel of data on air quality from 42 countries, they found a hump-shaped relation between some measures of air quality (such as $SO_2$ concentrations). Selden and Song (1994) found a similar pattern using data on sulfur dioxide ($SO_2$) emissions. This inverted-U pattern later came to be known as the Environmental Kuznets Curve (EKC) hypothesis: pollution emission first rises with the per capita income growth and, after a threshold level of income growth, it declines. This is illustrated in Figure 4.

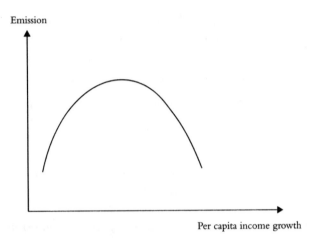

Emission

Per capita income growth

**FIGURE 4**  Environmental Kuznets Curve

But, for water quality indicators, empirical evidence of EKC is rather mixed. Three main categories of indicators are used as measures of water quality in the empirical studies. First, the concentration of pathogens in water like fecal and total coliforms; second, the amount of heavy metals like lead, cadmium, mercury, arsenic, and nickel, as well as toxic chemicals discharged in water by human activities; and third, the measure of deterioration of the water oxygen regime, such as dissolved oxygen, biological oxygen demand (BOD), and chemical oxygen demand (COD). While there is evidence of EKC for some indicators, the studies reach conflicting results about the shape and peak of the curve (Hettige et al. 2000). Different studies also estimate different turning points in the EKC relationship as reported in Table 5. As is evident from the Table, not only does the turning point vary across different pollutants, but also across different studies for the same pollutants.

The EKC derives its name from the work of Kuznets (1955), who postulated a similar relationship between income inequality and income growth. Growth, through industrialization, creates, as well as destroys jobs. Technological changes in a growing economy

**TABLE 5**  Estimated Turning Points in the EKC Relationship

| Pollutant | Study | Turning Point ($) |
|---|---|---|
| BOD | Grossman and Krueger (1995) | 7623 |
| COD | Grossman and Krueger (1995) | 7853 |
| $CO_2$ emissions | Selden and Song (1994) | 6241 |
|  | Cole et al. (1997) | 9900 |
| NOx emissions | Selden and Song (1994) | 12041 |
| SPM emissions | Selden and Song (1994) | 9811 |
|  | Cole (2003) | 7300 |
| $SO_2$ emissions | Selden and Song (1994) | 8916 |
|  | Cole (2003) | 8691 |

*Source*: Cole and Nuemayer (2005).

cause continuous changes in the composition of tech-
nologically upgrading and stagnant industries. These
changes generate as well as destroy productive employ-
ment opportunities. In the process, some people move
into the lower-income groups relative to where they
were at the beginning of the growth process (downward income mobility), and some people move into
the higher-income groups (upward income mobility).
At the initial phase of technological change, industrialization and growth, downward income mobility
becomes a predominant force, thereby raising income
inequality. Whereas only a handful of skilled workers can exploit new opportunities in the innovating
industries, the unskilled (low income) people who
are displaced cannot find gainful jobs elsewhere. But,
in the later stages, as the pace of industrial growth
slackens, such unfavourable forces become weaker,
and the income distribution pattern gets more even.
At the same time, benefits of income growth perme-
ate more widely to ensure lower inequality. More jobs
are created, both directly as well as indirectly, even for
the unskilled. On the other hand, with returns to skill
rising, more people pick up skills, and thus income
inequality falls.

The logic of the EKC relation is similarly intuitive and appealing. As Dasgupta et al. (2002) argue, in the first stage of industrialization, pollution grows rapidly because high priority is given to increasing material output, and people are more interested in jobs and income than in clean air and water. The rapid growth inevitably results in greater use of natural resources and emission of pollutants, which in turn puts more pressure on the environment. People, being at the lower level of the income ladder, disregard the environmental consequences of growth. In the later stage of industrialization, as income rises, people value the environment more, regulatory institutions become more effective, and pollution level declines. Thus, EKC hypothesis posits a well-defined relationship between the level of economic activity and environmental damage.

There are many other explanations of EKC as discussed in detailed surveys by Copeland and Taylor (2003) and Dinda (2004). We shall discuss some of the major explanations here. The most common explanation for the shape of an EKC is the idea that people attach increasing value to environmental quality when a country achieves a sufficiently high standard of living.

In fact, it posits an income elastic demand for environmental quality: after a particular level of income, the willingness to pay for a cleaner environment rises by a greater proportion than income. Copeland and Taylor (2003), in their survey on trade, growth, and the environment, on the other hand, reason that 'at low incomes, pollution rises with growth because increased consumption is valued highly relative to environmental quality. As income rises, the willingness to pay for environmental quality rises, and increasingly large sacrifices in consumption are made to provide greater environmental benefits'.

They further note that the EKC literature has provided 'quite convincing evidence that there is an income effect that raises the environmental quality. Moreover, there are strong indications that this income effect works because increases in the stringency of environmental regulation accompany higher per capita incomes'.

The other explanation for EKC runs in terms of the three effects discussed above. The inverted-U hypothesis implies that at low levels of income, the *scale* effect outweighs the *composition* and *technique* effects, creating a positive relation between income growth and environmental damage. At some higher level of income, however, the latter two effects outweigh the former. It is evident from this EKC that since freer trade raises income, it directly contributes to the growth-induced *scale* effect; but at the same time also induces the *composition* and *technique* effects of increased income. If a country is on the right side of the inverted-U, then freer trade will actually lower national pollution even if the country exports pollution-intensive goods. A similar outcome is expected for countries that grow faster so that they move over the inverted-U faster.

Andreoni and Levinson (2000) provide an interesting explanation for the EKC in terms of increasing returns in pollution abatement through adoption of cleaner technologies and cleaner production strategies. Their idea is that efficiency of pollution abatement may increase with its scale. These efficiencies make abatement more profitable, and hence pollution can fall as more abatement is undertaken even if pollution policy does not change. Copeland and Taylor (2003) observe that this explanation has an 'interesting twist on scale and technique effects because as the scale of output rises, even with constant pollution taxes, firms switch to cleaner techniques of production. The scale effect creates its own technique effect even with no pollution policy response to higher incomes'.

There have been quite a few studies that attempt to empirically test these alternative hypotheses for the EKC. Hettige, Mani, and Wheeler (2000), for example, attempted to isolate *composition* and *technique* effects, and explain how they vary with income. They use data on industrial water pollution from 12 countries. They found a hump-shaped relation between the share of manufactures and per capita income; however, they found this *composition* effect was small in magnitude relative to the impact of *scale* effects. On the other hand, they found a strong *technique* effect: the income elasticity of the pollution intensity is about−1, that is, 1 per cent growth in income brings about almost a proportionate decline in the pollution intensity of goods. Overall, they found that industrial water pollution tends to rise initially with income and then flatten out, with the strong *technique* effect being responsible for offsetting the *scale* effect of growth.

In a more recent study, Cole and Neumayer (2005) examine the implications of the EKC for the developing world. In particular, they investigate how long it will take for the developing world to reach the EKC turning point. Their findings are not very encouraging though as they predict that, even under very high growth scenarios, environmental quality is expected to worsen for many more years to come. This is in sharp contrast to an earlier optimistic observation by Dasgupta et al. (2002) that the EKC is flattening in the developing countries through increased formal and informal environmental regulations.

## The Chinese and East Asian Experience

In China, rapid economic growth exceeding 10 per cent per annum during the 1990s has also led to growth in industrial and municipal wastes, vehicle emissions, agricultural run-off, and deforestation. This has raised serious concerns regarding the sustainability of China's development path. It is estimated that eight out of the 10 most polluted cities in the world are located in China. Only 37 per cent of the surface water monitored meets the national standards, and less than 20 per cent of municipal wastewater is treated. As regards land degradation, 38 per cent of the land suffers from soil erosion, and 27 per cent from desertification. Different estimates of overall economic losses are also available. It is contended that, in recent years, economic losses by environmental damage amount in the range of 3.5–7.7 per cent of Chinese GDP, of which 59 per cent is caused by air pollution, and 36 per cent by water pollution.

During the 1990s, China gave increasing emphasis to the prevention of pollution emission, and shifted the responsibility to polluters to pay for environmental damage. A key policy instrument was a discharge fee system, with fees based on the concentration of effluents. These fees are applied to industrial emissions across China, with most revenue accruing from fees for discharges of wastewater and waste gases. But, it is widely believed, that the fees are only a fraction of the social cost of pollution, and that these fees do not encourage abatement. In the Tenth Five Year Plan (2001–5), the Chinese government stated explicit goals for the reduction of its water pollution, as measured by Chemical Oxygen Demand (COD), which is the mass concentration of oxygen consumed by chemical breakdown of organic and inorganic matter in water, and its air pollution, as measured by sulphur dioxide and other particulate matter, especially that generated by smoke and dust.

Using provincial level data on Chinese water pollution for 1987–95, Dean (2002) provides strong support for both a direct and an indirect effect of trade liberalization on emissions growth. She observes that these effects could be opposite in sign. It appears from this study that China has a comparative advantage in pollution-intensive goods, and thus increased openness directly aggravates environmental damage.

At the same time, increased openness strongly raises income growth. Income growth itself has a strong negative effect on emissions growth. Thus, trade liberalization indirectly mitigates environmental damage. A more recent study by Dean and Lovely (2008) provides further account and estimate of the impact of trade on environment in the Chinese economy. An interesting asymmetry in pollution intensity of exports and imports has been observed. Chinese exports are observed to be *less* water pollution intensive, and generally *less* air pollution intensive, than Chinese imports. However, both Chinese exports and imports are becoming cleaner over time. These cleaner trends in exports and imports are driven by both *composition* and *technique* effects, with the latter being the strongest.

The processing trade is observed to be cleaner than merchandise trade, and this largely explains the drop in pollution intensity of Chinese exports and imports over time. Thus, there seems to be a favorable *composition* effect generated by the increased fragmentation in Chinese trade. Another important factor contributing to China's cleaner exports, or the decline in the pollution intensity of China's exports observed by Dean and Lovely (2008), is its accession to WTO in the year 2001.

Matsuura and Takeda (2005), on the other hand, provide estimates of environmental pollution in 10 East Asian countries caused by trade with Japan and the USA. First of all, by calculating the specialization index of pollution-intensive industries during 1988–2000, they arrive at some interesting observations. For the poorest country in the region (by the per capita GDP measure), Vietnam, and for the Philippines, Japan was a net exporter of dirty goods. In the case of Indonesia, Malaysia and Thailand, Japan was a net exporter of dirty goods till mid-1990s, and then turned out to be a net importer. This reversal, according to Matsuura and Takeda (2005), is because of the industrialization process of these countries through foreign direct investment. A similar observation was made for trade between Japan and Korea. Finally, for the more advanced countries in the region—Singapore, Hong Kong, and Taiwan—which focused more on service and information technology intensive industries—Japan was a net exporter of dirty goods.

Second, considering air pollution as measured by $CO_2$ emissions, Matsuura and Takeda (2005) estimated the EKC relationship for East Asian countries to find two turning points. $CO_2$ emissions fall at very low levels of incomes and then rise to reach a peak

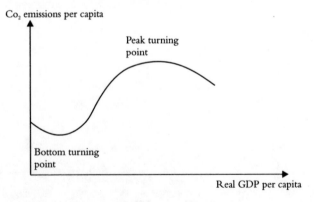

**FIGURE 5**  EKC for East Asian Countries

at very high levels of income before emissions start falling again. Thus, their empirical estimate generated an inverted N-shape relationship between income and $CO_2$ emissions for the East Asian countries. This is shown in Figure 5. Finally, they conclude that both domestic industrialization and increased exports of dirty goods to Japan raised $CO_2$ emissions in these East Asian countries. But, dirty trade with the USA did not affect pollution.

# 4

# Foreign Direct Investment, Capital Flight, and Pollution Haven

There are several dimensions to the relationship between foreign direct investment (FDI) and the environment in the host country. First is the argument that the environmental standard is an important determinant of capital flows across countries and FDI inflow in the developing countries. The twin hypotheses of capital flight and pollution haven characterize this dimension. A related issue is race-to-the-bottom, that is, competition amongst the developing countries through lowering of their environmental standards to attract FDI. These are the issues that concern the *cause* of FDI and migration of dirty industries from the developed to the developing countries. There are also issues concerning the *impact* of FDI on the environment in the host country, and *how* FDI impacts the environment through the *composition*, *scale*, and *technique* effects.

This chapter focuses on these dimensions, drawing heavily from surveys by Adams (1997), OECD (2002), and Jaffe et al. (1995). It documents evidence from case studies on some Latin American and Asian countries. Recent estimates of the impact of FDI inflow in India, for its air pollution measured by carbon dioxide ($CO_2$) and sulphur dioxide ($SO_2$) emissions, are reported in the concluding section.

## Pollution Havens and Capital Inflow

Over the last few decades, the developing countries have emerged as net exporters of dirty goods and the developed countries the net importers. Dirty industries have, in a sense, migrated to the developing countries. Of course, there are some region specific departures from this trend, as mentioned in Chapter 3 in the context of trade between Japan and the East Asian countries. Mani and Wheeler (1998) observed two general patterns in dirty-sector production trends for the Organization for Economic Co-operation and Development (OECD) economies since 1960. First, in all three regions—Japan, North America, and Western Europe—the share of pollution-intensive industries has significantly declined. Second, in Japan and North America, this decline has been accompanied by the net displacement of dirty good production to their relatively less developed trading partners. But for Western Europe, the trade balance has more or less been the same. Thus, it seems that whereas dirty industries may have migrated from Japan and North America, the pattern for Western Europe may not be as straightforward.

It is often argued that capital flight and the displacement of dirty industries can be explained by the differences in environmental standards across developed and developing countries. The awareness and demand for better environment in the rich and developed countries, which is itself related to income levels, as many studies have concluded, has raised the cost of operation of dirty industries there. Preference for faster output growth, on the other hand, often causes loose implementation of environmental standards in developing countries. With low per capita income, people have a lower preference for better environmental quality. There is, therefore, lesser political pressure on local governments to raise environmental standards. Accordingly, capital finds better and reliable returns in dirty industries in these countries than in the developed countries. This forms the basic premise of the capital flight hypothesis. The pollution haven hypothesis extends this argument further by postulating that developing countries deliberately keep their environmental standards low in order to attract foreign capital. That is, developing countries *choose* to remain pollution havens for dirty industries, thus ignoring environmental implications. The other implication of this hypothesis is that weak environmental standards in the developing countries establish their comparative advantages in dirty goods and enable them to export these goods. We will return to this aspect in the next chapter.

The pollution havens hypothesis goes even further by arguing that developing countries engage in active competition by lowering their environmental standards to attract foreign capital, thereby triggering a race-to-the-bottom. Theoretically, this makes sense if the weaker regulation alone attracts foreign capital. For example, consider a less-developed region comprising of two countries, A and B, having identical socio-economic, geographic, and political conditions. Suppose, capital inflow into this region from the outside world is fixed, say at US$ 1,000 million, and is equally shared by these two countries as long as these countries set the same environmental standard, high or low (see Box 10). But, if one country sets a lower environmental standard than the other, then the entire capital flows into that country. Clearly, for both these countries there will be a unilateral incentive to set a lower standard, and out-compete each other. The standards will, thus, be spiralling down in the region. The final outcome would be that both countries choosing the *same* lowest feasible standard, and thus having the same share of foreign capital as they would if they had set a very high (but the same) environmental standard. It is the foreign capital that gains at the cost of these countries. Both countries unambiguously lose from greater environmental damages due to the race-to-the-bottom. This unambiguously welfare-lowering Prisoners' Dilemma type of outcome is illustrated in Table 6 in terms of two standards—high and low. Each country has the choice of setting either the high or the low standard. The numbers in each cell indicate the country-share of the foreign capital inflow into this region. The first number is for country A and the second number is for country B. Note that in our construction, in the spirit of the pollution haven hypothesis that foreign capital flows into the country having weaker environmental regulations, when both choose the same standards—high–high or low–low—they get equal share. But all FDI flows into the country that sets a lower standard. Now, it is easy to check that for country A, it is always optimal to choose the low standard *regardless of what country B chooses*. For example, if country B chooses the high standard, country A attracts maximum foreign capital by setting the low standard. On the other hand, if country B chooses the low standard, country A gets a positive share of foreign capital if it chooses the same low standard and no share if it chooses the high standard. Hence, country A will always set the low standard. Similar reasoning shows that country B will

**TABLE 6**   Competition for Foreign Capital

| | | Country B | |
|---|---|---|---|
| | | High | Low |
| Country A | High | 500, 500 | 0, 1000 |
| | Low | 1000, 0 | 500, 500 |

also choose the low standard *regardless of what country A chooses*.

Note that the same outcome would have prevailed for country shares being $s$ and $(1-s)$ instead of 0 and 100 per cent for the high-standard and low-standard countries, respectively, with $s$ being strictly less than 50 per cent. Certainly the countries would have done better in terms of the environmental costs of attracting foreign capital if they could coordinate on setting the same high standard. Unfortunately, as the economic theory suggests, in the above kind of setting, such a coordinated outcome can never be sustained. We will return to similar kind of policy coordination problem in Chapter 6 and possible resolutions of this problem.

## Does Lax Standard Attract FDI?

The empirical evidence does not provide much support to the otherwise appealing pollution haven hypotheses. Developing countries have successfully attracted FDI inflows in the 1990s. Such flows aggregated an annual average of US$ 46 billion in the 1988–93 period. By 2000, this had grown to more than US$ 240 billion (UNCTAD 2003). The increasing trend in global FDI inflow continued even during 2000–7, with global inflows reaching its peak in 2007 at US$ 1,833 billion, surpassing the previous peak of 2000. The financial crisis that began in many countries in late 2007, however, slowed down this growth in the next two years. Drawing on the UNCTAD reported data, Figure 6 shows the trend in FDI inflow in the developing and the transition economies during 1970–2009. Transition economies, across which large variations in environmental standards have been observed, attract lowest FDI inflows for this country groups. On the

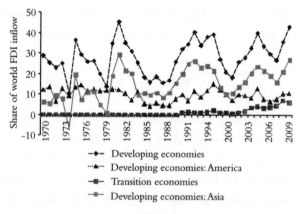

**FIGURE 6**   Share of World FDI Inflow by Country Groups
*Source*: Compiled from *UNCTAD Trade Statistics, 2011*.

other hand, since the mid-1980s, Asian developing countries have emerged as the largest recipients of FDI.

However, there are several caveats to this observation. First, it is true that the Asian countries, particularly the East Asian ones, have competed among themselves since 1990s to attract FDI under the notion that it is a necessary precondition for faster growth. Such competition has mostly been reflected in large unilateral tariff reductions to signal to the external world their more open trade and investment regimes. It is not clear, however, to what extent they competed in terms of lowering environmental regulations and taxes. Second, a large part of the FDI inflows in East Asian countries has been intra-region in character rather than from advanced industrialized countries of North America and Western Europe.

Third, such growing FDI inflow into the developing countries is due to a host of other factors. These include traditional determinants like low wages, large internal markets, availability of natural resources, and factors like favourable regulatory changes, local conditions facilitating the efficient operation of multinational corporations' technologies, and efficient management practices.

## Box 10   Prisoners' Dilemma

The Prisoners' Dilemma game is the best example of how unilaterally optimum acts of economic agents can actually make both worse off compared to what they could achieve if they could cooperate with each other. Following Luce and Raiffa (1957), consider two persons who are accused of committing two crimes, one minor for which they can be imprisoned without any proof for one year each, and the other major for which at least one of them must confess of committing the crime to be convicted. The prosecutor makes an offer to each of them in isolation that she will be freed of all charges if she only confesses whereas the other person will serve six years in jail. But if both confess, then each will be jailed for five years. The two persons have two options each: confess or not confess. The return to these strategies is shown in the following Table in terms of number of years of freedom each will get corresponding to their choices. Clearly, both could be better off if they could agree upon not confessing to the major crime. But, each will have unilateral incentive for confessing and thus getting free. Thus both will end up confessing and serving five years each in jail, that is, will gain only one year of freedom each.

|  | Payoffs of the Prisoners | | |
|---|---|---|---|
|  |  | Prisoner B | |
|  |  | Do not Confess | Confess |
| Prisoner A | Do not Confess | 5, 5 | 0, 6 |
|  | Confess | 6, 0 | 1, 1 |

Fourth, as Figure 7 reveals, except for the first half of the 1990s, among the Asian developing countries, the relatively high-income countries attract most of the FDI inflows. To the extent to which the demand for cleaner environment and, consequently, the demand for stricter environmental regulations increase with the per capita income level of a country, this does not suggest anything in favour of the capital flight hypothesis.

In their study, Mani and Wheeler (1998) noted that part of the shift in dirty good production from the OECD countries to their trade partners was 'probably due to low income elasticity of demand for pollution-intensive products'. Of course, stricter environmental regulation and rising abatement costs did appear to have played their part, but perhaps not significantly

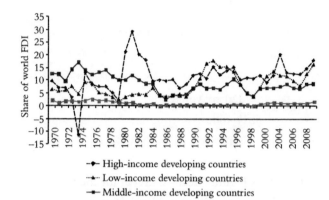

**FIGURE 7** Share of World FDI Inflow by Developing Countries and Income Category
*Source*: Compiled from *UNCTAD Trade Statistics, 2011.*

enough to provide support to the pollution haven hypothesis.

However, Xing and Kolstad (2002) show that the laxity of environmental regulations in a host country is a significant determinant of FDI from the US for heavily polluting industries, and is insignificant for less polluting industries. The heavily polluting industries are those with high pollution control costs, such as chemicals and primary metals. Less polluting industries, on the other hand, are those with more modest pollution control costs, such as electrical and non-electrical machinery, transportation equipment, and food products.

But, based on firm-level rather than industry-level data, Smarzynska and Wei (2004) found no support in favour of dirty industries migrating to developing countries in response to lax environmental standards there. They studied investment flows from multiple countries to 25 economies in Eastern Europe and the former Soviet Union. Choice of these transition countries was purpose-specific as they offer a large variation in terms of environmental standards. Smarzynska and Wei also took into account both the polluting intensity of the potential investor and the degree of environmental stringency in the potential host country. This allowed them to test whether dirty industries are relatively more attracted to locations with weaker standards. Despite these methodological improvements, they found no systematic evidence that FDI from 'dirtier' industries is more likely to go to countries with weaker environmental regulations.

Dean, Lovely, and Wang (2004), on the other hand, estimate the strength of pollution-haven behaviour by examining the location choices of 2,886 manufacturing equity joint venture (EJV) projects in China during 1993–6. They used data sets containing information on a sample of EJV projects, effective environmental levies on water pollution, and estimates of Chinese emissions and abatement costs for 3-digit International Standard Industrial Classification (ISIC) industries. Results show that provinces with high concentrations of foreign investment, relatively abundant stocks of skilled workers, concentrations of foreign firms, and special incentives attract EJVs from all source countries. Environmental stringency does affect location choice, but not in the manner and to the extent claimed by the pollution haven hypothesis. The EJVs with partners from Hong Kong, Macao, Taiwan, and other Southeast Asian developing countries are attracted by relatively weak environmental levies. But, joint ventures with partners from industrial country sources such as US, UK, and Japan are actually attracted by stringent environmental levies, regardless of the pollution intensity of the industry. Thus, it is not true that dirty industries migrate from the industrialized nations to the developing countries (at least in case of China) due to relatively less stringent environmental regulations in the latter.

## FDI Inflow and the Local Environment

Even if one doubts the validity of the pollution havens being the primary reason for large FDI inflow in the developing countries, such inflows per se may not be inconsequential for the local environment. Thus, a distinct body of research has emerged that examines not so much whether weak environmental standards are caused by FDI inflow, but whether the FDI inflow causes environmental degradation. The earlier analyses in this body of empirical literature are, however, at best inconclusive regarding effects of FDI on the pollution level in the host countries (Zarsky 1999). This inconclusiveness has, in recent years, shifted the focus of the research questions away from *whether* FDI is good or bad for the environment to about *when* FDI becomes beneficial for the host country environment.

Theoretically, FDI may have similar composition and scale effects, depending on the direction and nature of FDI flows. Of course, the composition effect is related to the question of whether FDI is attracted by lax environmental regulations. In many cases, particularly in the resource-based Latin American countries, FDI flows into mining, forestry, and fishing. This type of

FDI inflow has far-reaching adverse implications. But even if capital flows into all sectors of the economy, from the least to the most pollution-intensive production uniformly (thereby ruling out the pollution haven hypothesis a priori), the Rybczynski result discussed in Chapter 3, suggests that the capital-intensive sectors will expand more than the relatively labour-intensive ones. Thus, if dirty goods are relatively capital-intensive, FDI inflow changes the composition of aggregate output towards dirty goods.

On the other hand, to the extent to which FDI augments GDP growth of the host countries, there arises a scale effect, which is the indirect (and long run) adverse effect on host country pollution. Note that this adverse effect is the supply side phenomenon: growth raises economic activity all around and this, in turn, degrades the environment further. There is also the positive scale effect that arises when FDI augmented economic growth causes an increase in the demand for environmental goods and economic gains are used to tackle environmental problems. Thus, a favourable scale effect of FDI comes from the demand side.

The main argument of FDI being beneficial for the host country environment, on the other hand, is that foreign firms help improve the environmental performance in developing countries by transferring both cleaner technology and management expertise in controlling environmental impacts. This is the technique effect, which is mostly beneficial for the host country environment.

Haltia and Keipi (2000), for example, compare the net environmental benefits from forestry versus cattle farming investment in Chile and Brazil, concluding that forestry investments, especially pine and eucalyptus plantations, involve significantly larger environmental benefits than cattle farming. This suggests that scale effects are not only negative but also positive, especially when compared to other land use alternatives. The positive effects include prevention of soil erosion and $CO_2$ sequestration. But, in Brazil, forestry sector output has increased in the last two decades, both in timber, and especially in pulp and paper, which are highly pollution-intensive sectors. Borregaard, Dufey and Winchester (2008) attribute this increased *scale* effect largely to FDI inflow in these sectors. Eskeland and Harrison (2003), on the other hand, examined industry level FDI in four developing countries—Mexico, Cote d'Ivoire, Venezuela, and Morocco—and found

101

no significant positive correlation between industry level FDI and measures of air and water emissions.

In Asia, China is the largest recipient of FDI inflow from the world. In fact, almost one-third of FDI inflows from the world to the developing countries as a whole are being attracted by China. More than half of this FDI inflow comes from Hong Kong, Taiwan, Korea, and Singapore. Advanced industrialized countries as source of China's FDI inflow is still low—Japan, USA, UK, and Germany together accounting for only 24 per cent of Chinese FDI inflow. There has been some evidence of FDI enterprises involving the import of hazardous waste. For example, waste imported to China increased from 0.49 per cent of total imports in 1990 to 2.07 per cent in 1997, and most of the wastes came from developed countries and industrialized countries. But, overall, such large and growing inflow of FDI in China appears to have a positive impact on the local environment. This positive effect arises primarily from improved environmental management at the firm level. Recent estimates show that FDI flows into only about 40 per cent of pollution-intensive industries in China. On the other hand, Dean and Lovely (2008) observe that the FDI inflows

102

contributed to a decline in the pollution intensity of exports.

## The Indian Experience

FDI inflow in India has increased phenomenally since 1992 (see Figure 8). The increase has been particularly spectacular during 2004–9. The period of growth in FDI inflow has also coincided with India's trade and structural reforms and high rate of growth in its GDP. At the same time, though awareness for better environment is growing amongst the consumers, environmental taxes and standards are still, in many instances, less stringent than they should be. The questions that crops up then are whether the upsurge in capital inflow is caused by lax standards and how much damage these capital inflows are causing the environment.

A recent empirical study by Acharyya (2009) sheds some light on whether the pollution haven hypothesis can at all be a plausible explanation for FDI inflow in India. She looked at the sectoral distribution of FDI inflow in India and examined whether the share of dirty industries in aggregate FDI inflow increased during the 1990s. Adopting the conventional approach to

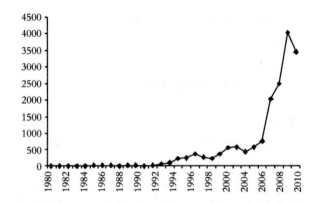

**FIGURE 8**    FDI Inflow in India (Mn US$)
*Source*: Compiled from *UNCTAD Trade Statistics, 2011.*

identify pollution-intensive sectors as those that incur
high levels of abatement expenditure per unit of output
in the USA and other OECD economies, she found
that among the highly polluting industries except for
Fuels, Transportation, and Chemicals, the FDI inflow
has been rather small during 1996–2003 (see Figure
9). FDI inflow has been even smaller in the cement
and gypsum industry which contributes almost 7 per
cent of world's air pollution through $CO_2$ emissions.
The $CO_2$ emission per capita by cement and gypsum
industry in India has increased from 0.14 metr c ton
in 1980 to 0.32 metric ton in 2003, according to

estimates of Carbon Dioxide Information Analysis Centre, Oak Ridge National Laboratory. But to what extent such an increase in $CO_2$ emission per capita can be attributed to FDI inflow into this sector is not known.

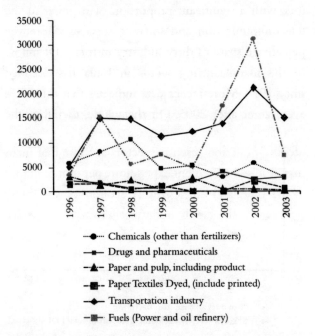

···●··· Chemicals (other than fertilizers)
─■─ Drugs and pharmaceuticals
─▲─ Paper and pulp, including product
─■─ Paper Textiles Dyed, (include printed)
─◆─ Transportation industry
─■─ Fuels (Power and oil refinery)

**FIGURE 9**   FDI Inflow in Some Selected Dirty Industries (Mn US$)

*Source*: Acharyya (2009).

Figure 10, on the other hand, illustrates the changing composition of FDI inflow across manufacturing and (relatively less or non-polluting) services and within the manufacturing industries. Almost one-third of FDI inflow is being attracted in the services sectors, with a significant proportion of it going to the telecommunication and software services. Moreover, percentage share of dirty industry in total FDI inflow to the manufacturing sector in India has declined since 1998. More recent data indicates that this fall is even larger after 2005. On the whole, therefore, the

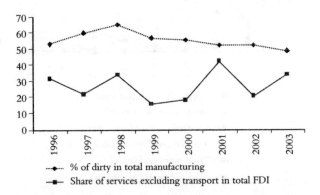

····•···· % of dirty in total manufacturing
——■—— Share of services excluding transport in total FDI

**FIGURE 10**  Share of Services and Dirty Manufacturing Industries in Total FDI (per cent share)
*Source*: Acharyya (2009).

106

pollution haven hypothesis does not appear to be a convincing argument behind FDI inflow in India, at least since the mid-1990s.

This does not mean, however, that FDI inflow did not cause any environmental damages. As Acharyya (2009) notes, this is because the pollution intensities and emission rates differ across different sectors. Moreover, FDI inflows may have multiplier effects on sectoral growth which may also differ significantly across the sectors due to asymmetries in the production and labour market conditions. Thus, even a small FDI inflow may have a large long run growth impact on the environment. To check this, she estimates the long run or growth effect of FDI inflow in India on the air pollution measured by $CO_2$ emissions. As illustrated in Figure 11, $CO_2$ emission per capita has grown steadily over the period 1970–2005. To examine to what extent this rising $CO_2$ emission can be attributed to the growth effect of FDI, she carries out a two-stage co-integration estimation. In the first stage, the impact of FDI inflow on growth is estimated, and then the impact of such FDI-induced GDP growth on $CO_2$ emission is estimated. The empirical estimates reveal that there has been a stable long run positive growth

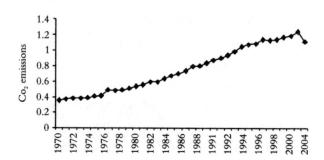

**FIGURE 11**   $CO_2$ Emissions (metric tonnes per capita)
*Source:* Acharyya (2009).

impact of FDI inflow in India on $CO_2$ emissions during 1980–2003. More precisely, the FDI inflow in India raises $CO_2$ emission by 0.86 per cent for every 1 per cent growth in GDP that such inflow contributes to.

Baek and Koo (2008) have found similar evidence of adverse growth effect of FDI on $SO_2$ emissions in India. As they observed, with the large FDI inflow and significant GDP growth, $SO_2$ emissions in India has increased by almost 110 per cent between 1980 and 2000. The short run dynamics studied by them reveal that both economic growth and $SO_2$ emissions in India are significantly affected by the inflow of FDI.

# 5

# Environmental Regulation, Comparative Advantage, and Unfair Trade

An interesting dimension of the pollution haven hypothesis discussed in the previous chapter, which has raised considerable debate and constituted the bone of contention between the developed and the developing world, is its implication for the pattern of trade and exports of the developing countries. Lower environmental standards in the developing countries, compared to the developed nations, generates a comparative advantage for them in dirtier goods and, therefore, boosts their exports of such goods to the developed world. The developing countries, it is contended, thus engage in *unfair* trade. Further, environmentalists are concerned that if countries with stricter regulations engage in free trade with countries with weaker regulations, the standards may be lowered in the former countries, due to political pressures to protect their own industries. Developing countries, on the other hand, construe the motivation of restricting trade through environmental regulations imposed on imports from them as a non-tariff barrier in disguise. They think of it as a ploy to protect domestic industries in the richer countries. There are several theoretical and empirical caveats to these arguments, which this chapter focuses upon.

## Environmental Standards and Comparative Advantage

Pethig (1976) was the first to float the idea that countries with a relatively weak environmental policy will specialize in dirty industry production, and thus export polluting goods. Later, Chichilnisky (1994) assumed exogenous differences in the property rights regime as a source of comparative advantage in dirty goods. Usually, poor countries do not assign any property rights to environmental resources, while rich countries do. As a result, poor countries gain a comparative advantage in dirty goods that take environmental resources as free inputs.

This type of comparative advantage is fundamentally different from the advantage derived from fundamental sources—factor endowment difference, technology asymmetry, and taste biases. The latter type of comparative advantage rests on the strength of an economy in a particular line of production—strength, either in terms of relative labour productivity or in terms of the relative availability of a factor that is used more intensively in that line of production. These are cases of genuine comparative advantage. On the other hand, a comparative advantage generated by the environmental factor does not rest on the strength of the economy, rather on the weakness of the economy. It is an outcome of the failure of the country to protect its environmental resources. It is a *perverse* comparative advantage, which arises from the undervaluation of the social cost of production.

It is important here to note that as long as we consider inter-industry trade in non-differentiated goods, arbitrage is the key force behind international trade, and for this there must exist cross-country differences in *pre-trade* prices. However, price differences are the only manifestation of the basis of trade. Such price differences arise due to many factors. For example, there can be a supply bias emanating from technology asymmetry. To illustrate, as an example of genuine comparative advantage, how cross-country difference in production technologies create a supply bias and result in differences in pre-trade (relative) market prices, consider our two-country, two-good world. In Figure 12 below, the relative demand for dirty good (which is the ratio of quantity demanded of dirty good per unit of quantity demanded of the clean good) and relative supply of dirty good (which is the ratio of units of dirty good produced per unit of the clean good being produced) are shown for our Home and Foreign countries. We have drawn the same relative demand curve $d$ for both the countries. That means we assume there is no demand bias across the countries for the dirty good (relative to the clean good). This is the case when tastes are homothetic and identical across our Home and Foreign countries. Essentially, this rules out the *income* effect on the demand for environmental quality that we have mentioned earlier and allows us to focus only on the supply side of the argument.

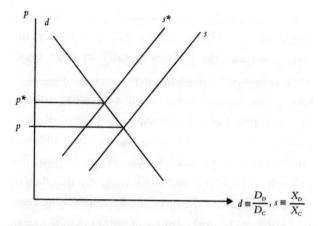

**FIGURE 12** Technology and Comparative Advantage in Dirty Good

However, suppose the Foreign country has superior technology in producing the clean good relative to the Home country. Then the Foreign country will be producing the clean good at a lower cost-price than the Home country. Put the other way, the relative cost of producing the dirty good will be lower at Home than in the Foreign country. Thus, the relative Home supply curve $s$ will lie below (or to the right of) the relative Foreign supply curve $s^*$. This supply bias creates the scope for arbitrage as the pre-trade relative price of the dirty good in the Home country is lower than

113

that in the Foreign country at the respective 'autarchic equilibria'. The Home country thus specializes in the dirty good and the Foreign country in clean good. This comparative advantage, however, is genuine as its source lies in technology asymmetry across nations. Similar supply bias and, consequently, pattern of comparative advantage, can arise if countries have different endowments of primary factors of production. For example, if the Home country is relatively abundant in physical capital and the dirty good requires more capital (relative to labour) per unit of output than the clean good, then the Home country will produce relatively more of the dirty good (and less of the clean good) than the Foreign country. Once again, the relative supply curve of the Home country will lie to the right of that of the Foreign country. Given identical and homothetic tastes, the relative price of the dirty good will be lower in the Home country than in the Foreign country. In both these cases, the sources of comparative advantage in dirty good for the Home country lie in its relative strength—technology in the former case and capital abundance in the latter.

The story of pollution havens specializing in and exporting dirty goods can now be put into this framework in several ways. Dirty goods damage the environment and inflict utility losses for the society. Private producers do not internalize this in their estimate of cost. A typical example is industrial pollution emission causing health hazards and thus raising the health care expenditure of inhabitants in the surrounding area who breathe the polluted air. Similarly, a chemical plant pollutes the water by putting chemical wastes in a river, which adversely affects the fish population in the river. This, in turn, affects the livelihood of fishermen who depend on the catch of fish in the river. These are the classic cases of negative externality whereby social costs exceed the private costs of production. As a result of the underestimation of the social cost, the producers over-produce. A standard socially optimal solution in such cases of negative externalities is to impose production taxes to the extent of the difference between social and private marginal costs. Essentially, the idea is to force the producers to internalize the costs that they inflict on others through taxes. Alternatively, the local agency can force the firms to comply with environmental norms and undertake pollution abatement efforts through a system of penalty.

Given this perspective, consider Figure 13 where the curve labelled $s$ represents the ratio of social marginal cost of producing the dirty good to that of the clean good. The curve labeled $s_p$ represents the ratio of private marginal cost of producing the dirty good to that of the clean good. For the clean good, private and social marginal costs are the same. But for the dirty good, the social marginal cost is larger than the private marginal cost for reasons just spelled out. Hence, the curve $s$ lies wholly above the curve $s_p$. The divergence between these cost ratios increases with the relative supply of the dirty good because of the *congestion* or *volume effect*. Suppose the Home and Foreign countries are identical in the sense that there are no demand and supply biases in the fundamentals. That is, suppose the two countries have identical tastes and have identical technology and factor endowments to produce the goods. But, whereas the Foreign country strictly enforces the environmental regulation and thus forces the firms to internalize the external costs that they inflict upon the environment while producing the dirty good, the Home country does not impose any such regulations. Thus, in the Foreign country, producers operate along $s$ and in the Home country

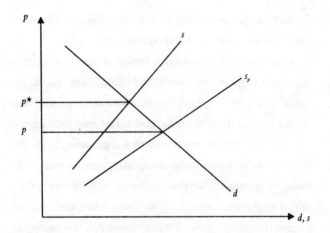

**FIGURE 13** Weak Environmental Standards and Export of Dirty Good

producers operate along $s_p$. It follows that the pre-trade relative price of the dirty good would be higher in the Foreign country and lower in the Home country where there is no environmental tax or regulation. A comparative advantage in the dirty good arises for the Home country not because of any difference in factor endowment, technology, or taste but because of the difference in environmental standards. This is the basis of the bone of contention between the developed and developing countries. To the extent to which

117

fundamentals are similar, the developing countries are therefore engaged in unfair trade.

This case is also termed as *ecological dumping*: a comparative advantage in a *dirty* good that arises due to lax environmental standards or inadequate taxation that allows it to be priced below the social marginal cost.

There are a few caveats to this argument, however. First, ex post, looking at the cross-country price differences it would be premature to talk about either unfair trade or ecological dumping. As illustrated in Figure 12 above, the Home country's comparative advantage may be purely due to technological reasons or a reflection of relative factor abundance. Even if the Home country had strictly enforced its environmental regulations and thereby forced its producers to abate pollution, technology asymmetry (or any other similar fundamental difference) could have still caused a supply bias in the dirty good for the Home country.

Second, as long as environmental standards are set optimally, cross-country differences in them may be a reflection of structural differences of countries rather than pollution havens. This has been well argued in Copeland and Taylor (1994) and Bhagwati and Srinivasan (1996). Copeland and Taylor (1994) demonstrate that endogenous income-induced policy differences both create, and, respond to, trade. Thus, whereas initial income differences across rich and poor nations explain policy differences, income changes induced by international trade changes this policy difference further. Bhagwati and Srinivasan (1996: 166), on the other hand, categorically point out that 'optimal pollution taxes ... will not be equal across countries: diversity in these tax rates will be both natural and appropriate, hence also legitimate'.

Third, which is in fact related to the first caveat, in the case where a comparative advantage still would have existed for the poor countries after strict enforcement of environmental regulations, the richer nations' clamour for uniform environmental standards is often perceived as their ploy to use these standards as non-tariff barriers to protect their own producers.

Fourth, as Copeland and Taylor (2003) demonstrate, trade need not induce dirty industry migration from rich to poor countries; rather there can be a reverse migration. Note that though we have dealt with different sources of comparative advantage—fundamental or policy generated—separately (under *ceteris paribus* assumption) in Figures 12 and 13, in real worlds countries may differ from each other in all these dimensions or sources. The comparative advantage is, thus, the outcome of the interaction of these differences. For example, advanced industrialized and richer countries are relatively better endowed in physical as well as human capital relative to the poorer nations. Historically, richer nations also have stricter environmental regulations than the poorer nations. Thus, to the extent to which the dirty good is relatively capital-intensive, capital abundance of the richer nations create a supply bias of dirty good for them. Stricter regulations in the rich countries, on the other hand, create a supply bias of the same for the poorer nations. If the rich nations are too rich in capital, we can expect the supply bias for the richer nations to be stronger. The end result is that, the richer nations will specialize in and export dirty goods to the poorer nations. Therefore, trade shifts dirty good production from the country with weak pollution regulation (poor nations) to the country where regulations are more stringent (rich nations). As Copeland and Taylor (2003) point out, this *global composition effect* reduces global pollution because dirty industries migrate to countries with higher standards and, thus, are forced to adopt cleaner techniques and higher abatement costs than they would have in poor nations. This is in sharp contrast with the pollution haven hypothesis that trade raises global pollution by shifting dirty good production to the countries with weak regulations.

## Evidence on Pollution Havens and Unfair Trade

Most of the empirical evidence provides very little support for the pollution haven hypothesis that weak environmental regulations establish comparative advantage for the developing countries in dirty goods, and thus dirty industries migrate from the developed to the developing world. In one of the earliest works on pollution havens, Tobey (1990) tested whether domestic environmental regulations have an impact on international trade pattern in five pollution-intensive industries for 23 countries. He found no statistical significance of his environmental regulation measures on the net exports of these industries. A similar conclusion was reached by Grossman and Krueger (1993) who examined the environmental impacts of NAFTA. They found no evidence that a comparative advantage is being created by lax environmental regulations in Mexico. But, using data across different countries from 1960–95, Mani and Wheeler (1998) found that pollution haven effects are insignificant in developing countries because production is mainly for domestic consumption, not for export. Their analysis also suggests that stricter environmental regulation had a significant impact on Japan's comparative advantage in pollution-intensive products. It led to significant abatements by pollution-intensive industries in Japan, and the displacement of some pollution-intensive production to Japan's trading partners.

Interestingly, their analysis sheds some light on the theoretical possibility mentioned above: that difference in environmental regulations may be outweighed by other natural cost advantages so that dirty industries may migrate to regions with stricter environmental regulations. There has been a steady decline of pollution-intensive industry in Japan since the mid-1960s. Relative to Japan and Western Europe, North America has a lower settlement density (and land prices), a much greater supply of bulk raw materials, and substantially lower energy prices. All these factors would enhance comparative advantage in pollution-intensive products in North America and compensate for its higher abatement expenses. It also has a skilled labour force capable of rapid adjustment toward cleaner production processes. It is, therefore, possible that the pollution-intensive production is displaced from Japan and Western Europe to North America. But North America's import/export ratio has increased steadily during the last two decades-and-a-half of the last century, and this indicates that the North American experience was actually quite similar to that of Japan.

For 21 OECD countries for the year 1992, van Beers and van den Bergh (1997) test the hypothesis that countries having strict environmental regulations experience relatively low levels of exports and relatively high levels of imports. They find no significant effect of the environmental policy stringency on dirty export flows. This, they infer, is because most of the dirty industries are resource-based. On the other hand, a significant negative effect of the environmental policy stringency is found for non-resource-based activities. In another study, Xu (2000) examines whether more stringent domestic environmental policies reduce the international competitiveness of environmentally sensitive goods (ESG) for 34 countries from 1965 to 1995. Among these countries were the OECD countries (excluding Czech Republic, Hungary, Iceland, and Turkey) and major East Asian developing economies. The time series evidence indicates that there are no systematic changes in trade patterns of ESGs since the 1970s, despite the introduction of more stringent environmental regulations in most of the developed countries since then. Econometric exercises also suggest that countries with more stringent environmental regulations do not reduce their exports of ESGs and non-resource-based ESGs.

The study by Akbostancý et al. (2004), on the other hand, examines the Turkish manufacturing industry for the period of 1994–7. These authors develop pollution indices based on industrial waste output data to measure industrial dirtiness. Estimation results using such pollution indices indicate that pollution intensity of different industries seems to be a determinant of Turkish exports. Thus, this analysis provides some evidence for the trade effect of the pollution haven hypothesis for Turkey.

# Government Policy and
# Two-way Causality

Antweiler et al. (2001) argues that trade and environmental policy are linked via the government's policy
process and, thus, most of the above cited empirical
analyses miss the fact that imports and pollution abatement costs are determined simultaneously. There are
two possible links between trade and environmental
policy. The first kind of link is in the context of political motive choice of government policies. Suppose
a tariff cut on dirty goods imports hurts factors
specific to the polluting industries, then political pressure may prompt the local government to compensate
these factors by weakening environmental regulation
after trade liberalization occurs. Thus, imports rise by
less than expected, and pollution abatement costs are
lower than expected. This argument, in fact, echoes the
environmentalists' concern mentioned at the beginning
of this chapter: free trade with countries having weaker
environmental standards and regulations will force the
developed country governments to lower standards as
well, under domestic political pressures.

A large country that can influence its terms of trade through changes in its policies suggests the second possible link between trade and environment (see Box 11). It is well known that a large country gains from imposing tariffs on its imports. Thus, a dirty good importer, if it is large (not in the geographical sense but as buyer and seller of traded goods), has an incentive to impose an optimal tariff to improve its terms of trade. But, if a negotiated tariff reduction takes place—for example in the context of multilateral negotiations at the WTO or regional integration—then the government has an incentive to look for an alternative instrument to manipulate the terms of trade in its favour. Relaxing its pollution regulations will provide an implicit subsidy to its domestic polluting industry and therefore can be a useful, though a second best, instrument to generate benefits from trade. This kind of policy response once again leads governments to lower pollution taxes when imports rise, and raise pollution taxes when exports rise.

If the tariff imposing country had been small, that is, an insignificant buyer and seller in the world market, by imposing tariffs it could not shift the terms of trade in its favour. Its real income would then have

BOX 11   Optimal Trade Policy for a Large Country

It is well demonstrated by Harry G. Johnson, among others, that if a trading nation is large in the sense that it is a significant buyer of its imports and significant seller of its exports in the world market, then it can do better by imposing tariffs on its imports rather than allowing them free. At initial world prices, tariffs on imports raise their domestic prices and thus lower import demand. If the tariff imposing country is large, such decline in import demand lowers world prices. There is, thus, a terms of trade improvement for the large tariff-imposing country. The welfare or real income improves on this account. At the same time, as tariffs lower the volume trade, the welfare or real income declines. For small tariff levels, the terms of trade effect is larger than the volume of trade effect, so that the country experiences a net real income gain. But, as tariffs are raised successively, the volume of trade effects become larger and beyond a particular level of tariff, the real income starts falling till a prohibitively high tariff chokes off all trade and the real income falls to the pre-trade level. This inverted-U relation between tariff levels and the real income of a large country is shown in Figure 14. A welfare maximizing policymaker thus should choose the strictly positive level of tariff $t_{opt}$ rather than a zero tariff (or free trade).

127

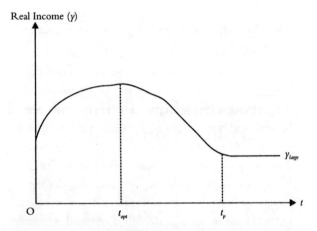

**FIGURE 14** Tariff as Optimal Trade Policy for a Large Country

unambiguously declined with the volume of trade. Free trade, thus, is the optimal (or welfare maximizing) policy for a small country.

# 6

# Trans-boundary Pollution and Policy Coordination

The discussions of various facets of environmental damages and their causes, in the previous chapters, have considered pollution that is localized, or the impact of which is confined within a small geographical area and political boundary of a nation. But, more often than not, environmental damage spreads over a very large geographical area that overlaps with more than one political boundary. In some cases, pollution originating in one country transmits to other countries. In other cases, the environment or atmosphere that overlaps with political boundaries of more than one country is degraded by economic activities by the same set of nations. Both are the cases of trans-boundary pollution. The dimension of the problem, however, is different in the two cases. In the former case, the trans-boundary pollution is *unidirectional*, involving one polluter and one or more polluted nations. In the latter, the same set of countries is polluter as well as victim, and thus the trans-boundary pollution is *regional reciprocal* in nature. In this case, it is difficult to delineate the polluter from the victim. In both these cases, abating trans-boundary pollution requires policy regulations of a supranational nature. Essentially, the negative externality in case of trans-boundary pollution is global rather than national in nature. Thus, nationally optimum policies are no longer the best way to resolve the problem. Policy coordination amongst countries is needed to take care of the global externality problem. But such policy coordination, as we will show, cannot be sustained without a supranational authority or a rule of reciprocation.

This chapter elaborates upon the different types of trans-boundary pollution, their implications, and the policy coordination problem.

## Trans-boundary Pollution: Nature and Dimension

Trans-boundary pollution is pollution that originates in one country and is then transmitted to other countries through pathways of water or air, and thereby causes damage to the environment of other countries. That is, economic activity organized in one country causes damage to the environment in that country as well as in other countries.

As mentioned earlier, trans-boundary pollution can be of several types. It can be unidirectional, regional reciprocal, or global. The most common example of unidirectional trans-boundary pollution where the polluter and the victim can be easily identified is water pollution transmitted through rivers that flow through more than one country. As a river flows through several countries, water pollution originating in upstream countries transmits to the downstream countries, causing health hazards and other environmental problems in the downstream countries. For example, the Ganges flowing through India and Bangladesh, carries water pollution caused by chemical plants, leather manufacturing units, and other industrial units in India through to Bangladesh. This is a case where we have one polluter (India) and one victim (Bangladesh). But there can be more than one polluter and more than one victim. Take for example The Nile and its tributaries that flow through nine countries. The White Nile

131

flows though Uganda, Sudan, and Egypt. The Blue Nile starts in Ethiopia and its tributaries pass through Zaire, Kenya, Tanzania, Rwanda, and Burundi before flowing into the Nile or into lake Victoria Nyanes. The Blue Nile joins the White Nile in Sudan and then goes into the Mediterranean Sea. In this case, Uganda and Ethiopia are the two extreme upstream countries, whereas the others are downstream countries relative to these two but upstream countries relative to each other according to their geographical location. Thus, a country like Sudan is both polluter as well as victim of trans-boundary water pollution carried through the Nile.

The other most common example of trans-boundary pollution is $CO_2$ emission, which is actually a global pollutant. Long-distance transport of airborne particles also has been documented around the world. For example, dust from the Gobi Desert of Mongolia travels far out into the Pacific Ocean. A Japanese research group in 1971 observed dust particles moving to Hawaii and Alaska through the atmosphere over Japan. They concluded that a single surge of dust from the Gobi had drifted across the Pacific for well over 10,000 kilometres.

The contamination of the Arctic marine food web by organochlorine compounds (OCs) is now a well-known phenomenon. Organochlorine compounds include pesticides such as lindane, chlorodane, toxaphene, polychlorinated biphenyls (PCBs), and the like. Many of these compounds, which have been banned in North America and Western Europe since the late 1970s, are still being emitted into the environment in many parts of the world. For example, toxaphane is still sprayed on crops in India and China. Heavy metals, on the other hand, are produced mainly by smelting, burning of fossil fuels, and waste incineration. Most of the organochlorine compounds detected at southern latitudes have also been detected in the Arctic. Since the Arctic has few local sources of pollution, most of the contaminants affecting it have travelled many miles from low and mid-latitude sources. Once released into the environment, they reach the Arctic through the atmosphere, rivers, and ocean water currents.

Regional reciprocal trans-boundary pollution, on the other hand, arises when a common property resource is polluted by several countries. All countries having access to this common property resource are the polluter as well as the victims. The most common example is the degradation of the European atmosphere and acid rain. Sulphur oxides are emitted into the atmosphere when fossil fuel is burnt by the European countries, which are transformed into sulphates and are transported long distances from the source by the winds. Since winds blow in several directions, the transportation of sulphates in the atmosphere is not unidirectional. These sulphates are finally deposited on the soil far from the source country through rain. When sulphur oxides are emitted for sufficiently long periods of time, this results in acid rain damaging the soil, surface water, and forestry. Sometimes this type of trans-boundary pollution is also labelled as global pollution because of several source countries for such emissions.

## Trade, Trans-boundary Pollution, and Pollution Content Tariff

Trade contributes to larger trans-boundary pollution in the same ways as it contributes to national pollution levels. The estimation and quantification of pollution that spills over to other geographical locations from the source location due to trade, however, is a difficult empirical task. $CO_2$ being a global or trans-boundary pollutant, one can provide gross estimates of $CO_2$ emissions and, therefore, trans-boundary pollution generated by trade-induced production increases. But, it is not easy to separate out how much of that emission actually transmits to neighbouring countries. The task is even harder in the case of regional reciprocal trans-boundary pollution such as the acid rain mentioned before, where it is difficult to estimate contribution of each polluter to sulphur emission into atmosphere and latter deposition of such emissions in different countries.

Even when quantification is possible, and the exact magnitude of trans-boundary pollution transmitted by an exporting country to an importing country can be estimated, trade restrictions are not in the best interest of the importing country, as spelled out earlier. To reiterate, a pollution content tariff, for example, restricting imports from the polluting country, comes at a cost as the importing country loses some of the gains from trade that it could have realized without such a tariff. However, Copeland (1996) argued that if the exporting country regulates its pollution emission, the importing country may have an incentive to impose a pollution-content tariff. To exemplify, consider an upstream Foreign country and a downstream Home country trading two goods with each other—chemical products, and cloth. The chemical product is produced only in the Foreign country and cloth is produced only in the Home country. Thus, under this extreme assumption, the Foreign country exports the chemical product, which it does not consume as well, in exchange for cloth from the Home country. The chemical product generates water pollution that transmits to the downstream Home country through the river flowing through these two countries. Suppose cloth production and consumption do not generate any pollution. There are other goods that are being produced and consumed locally in the two countries which also do not generate any kind of pollution. Thus, we have a case of unidirectional trans-boundary water pollution generated by international trade. The import demand for the chemical product in the Home country, thus, can essentially be interpreted as demand for pollution. Larger the demand for the chemical product, larger is the demand for pollution since by the scale effect a larger output should mean larger trans-boundary pollution. The local government at the Home country can lower the trans-boundary pollution through a pollution content tariff on imports of chemical product from the Foreign country. On the other hand, the local government in the Foreign country can abate the pollution level transmitted to the Home country through issuing a pollution permit to the producers of chemical products at a price (or tax) $\tau^*$. A higher price of the pollution permit feeds into the cost of production and raises the price of the chemical product. This lowers the import demand for chemical product in the Home country and hence the demand for pollution. Thus, the demand for pollution varies inversely with the price of the pollution permit in the foreign country. This is shown by the curve $DZ_o$ in Figure 15.

In the absence of any pollution permit or pollution quota in the Foreign country, the maximum pollution transmitted to the Home country is $Z_o$. Suppose, the local government in the Foreign country reduces trans-boundary pollution through a pollution quota that restricts pollution level at $\overline{Z}$. The price for the pollution permit or quota that the local producers of chemical products in the Foreign country pay to their government is $O\tau_o^*$. The government thus extracts a rent or revenue equal to the area $O\tau_o^* a\overline{Z}$ from the

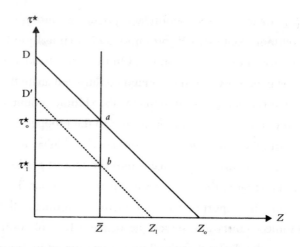

**FIGURE 15** Trans-boundary Pollution and Pollution-content Tariff

producers through the pollution permit. Now, if the Home country imposes a pollution-content tariff on imports of chemical products, the demand curve shifts to the left to $D'Z_1$ and the producers pay a lower price $O\tau_1^*$ for the permit. Part of the quota rent measured by the area $\tau_1^* ba\tau_o^*$ is now transferred to the Home country and this provides an additional incentive for the local government there, to impose a pollution-content tariff.

# Regional Reciprocation, Trans-boundary Pollution, and Policy Coordination

The main implication of trans-boundary pollution is that the externality generated by polluting activities, production or consumption, is no longer limited to one particular country (the polluter), but is of a regional or global nature. This makes policy intervention in this context a supranational one. Note that nationally optimum environmental regulations to abate trans-boundary pollution are sub-optimal. This is because such policies do not take into account environmental costs inflicted upon other countries. Thus, policy coordination among European countries in abating sulphur emission in the European atmosphere, or among African countries contributing to and suffering from the polluted water of the Nile, is necessary to optimally abate trans-boundary pollution in each case. But, this is hard to attain without any supranational regulatory authority enforcing policy cooperation or coordination, or without any rules of reciprocation that induces countries to cooperate.

Maler (1992) formalized this policy coordination problem in the context of trans-boundary or global pollution. Suppose there are $n$ countries contributing to sulphur emissions in the atmosphere, and that the amount of sulphur deposition (through acid rain) in a country contributed by its own emissions and by emissions by other countries is estimable. In particular, let $a_{ij}$ be the amount of sulphur deposited in country-$j$ from one unit of sulphur emission by country-$i$. Similarly, let $a_{ii}$ be the amount of sulphur deposited in country-$i$ from its own emission of one unit of sulphur. Also let $d_i$ denote the level of sulphur deposited in country-$i$. Now consider the regulatory policy of country-$i$ that sets a target level of pollution abatement, $E_i$. There is a cost to pollution abatement that increases with the target level of abatement and this is denoted by $C_i(E_i)$. The benefit from pollution abatement, on the other hand, is the environmental damage that can be *avoided*, which depends on the sulphur deposition, $D_i(d_i)$. A unilaterally national optimum level of pollution abatement is one that maximizes the *damage avoided* from its own emission, $a_{ii}D_i(d_i)$, less the pollution abatement cost. That is, the nationally optimum $E_i$ thus chosen does not take into account the benefits that other countries could have obtained from emission abatement as measured by $a_{ij}D_i(d_i)$ $\forall j \neq i$. Hence, there will be under-abatement of pollution emission compared to the globally optimum level.

Figure 16 illustrates this under-abatement when countries unilaterally decide about their respective levels of trans-boundary abatement. The marginal damage in country-$i$ from its own emission is shown by the downward sloping curve: marginal damage declines with the level of emission abated. The nationally optimum pollution abatement level will therefore be the level for which the marginal damage from own emission and marginal abatement cost are exactly equal to each other. For a lower level of abatement, the marginal damage avoided exceeds the marginal cost and thus it makes sense to raise the abatement level. For a higher level of abatement, on the other hand, the marginal damage avoided is lower than the marginal cost and thus the net benefit can be raised by lowering the abatement level.

However, the total damage caused that can be avoided through pollution abatement by country-$i$ is larger because of the trans-boundary nature of the pollution. The curve labelled $\Sigma MD_i$ represents the sum of such marginal damages. Thus, globally optimal level of pollution abatement for country-$i$ is $E_i^C$. The countries,

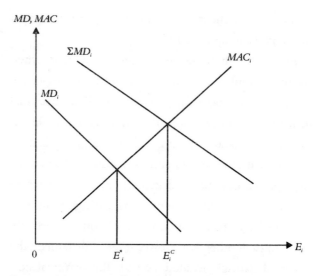

**FIGURE 16** Nationally Optimum and Cooperative Abatement Levels

while unilaterally choosing their pollution abatement levels, will never set this level and, thus, a framework for policy coordination or cooperation is required, whereby all countries choose the higher level of abatement $E_i^C$. However, in the absence of any supranational regulatory authority or rules of reciprocation, this policy coordination is not possible. To see why, suppose all countries agree to implement this globally optimal level of abatement. But for any country there would be *unilateral* incentive for defecting from this agreement. Note that if country-$i$ defects and implements the nationally optimal level of pollution abatement $E_i^*$, it can save upon the pollution abatement cost for additional level of pollution abatement under the cooperative agreement, $E_i^C - E_i^*$. On the other hand, it benefits from other countries abiding by the agreement and abating the higher cooperative level of pollution abatement as that would mean less sulphur emission in the atmosphere and consequently less sulphur deposition in country-$i$. Thus, country-$i$ gains by defecting from the cooperation when others honour the agreement. The same incentive for unilateral defection exists for all other countries. Hence, *all countries will defect*, each expecting that every other country will implement the cooperative level of pollution abatement. Cooperation will thus fail and the countries as a whole will be worse off since total marginal damage from sulphur emission and deposition in the region will be higher than if they could cooperate to implement the $E_i^C$ level of pollution abatement.

Thus, a supra-national authority is required to enforce the (regionally) optimum cooperative level of pollution abatement. The regional trading blocs like ASEAN, the EU, MERCOSUR, and NAFTA often act as the supranational authorities to the resolution of the policy coordination problem *regionally*. Linking environmental issues to trade gains and losses can resolve the environmental Prisoners' Dilemma. A detailed discussion is also available in Sanyal and Acharyya (2001). In fact, broader environmental issues are linked with mutual trade liberalization and cooperation among the member countries. There are quite a few examples of this: the MERCOSUR treaty amongst Argentina, Brazil, Paraguay, and Uruguay links environmental issues with mutual trade liberalization; accession of Mexico to the NAFTA was conditioned by resolving trans-boundary pollution problems between the USA and Mexico, requiring the latter to implement stricter regulations and higher level of pollution abatement. Another example is the ASEAN Cooperation plan, which is elaborated in the next section.

Enforcing the cooperative level of pollution abatement through regional trading arrangements has limited geographical coverage since the trading blocs do not always overlap. Moreover, not all trading blocs have the legal authority to enforce sanctions against the defecting sovereign member states.

## ASEAN Cooperation Plan

An example of tying up environmental issues with gains from regional agreements on trade is the ASEAN Cooperation plan. The ASEAN Ministers for the Environment on 19 June 1990 adopted the Kuala Lumpur Accord on Environment and Development aiming at 'the harmonization of trans-boundary pollution prevention and abatement practices'. This was followed by the Singapore Declaration issued at the conclusion of the Fourth Meeting of the ASEAN Heads of Government held on 27–8 January 1992. This declaration stated that 'ASEAN member countries should continue to enhance environmental cooperation, particularly in issues of trans-boundary pollution, natural disasters, forest fires and in addressing the anti-tropical timber campaign'.

With the worsening impact of trans-boundary pollution in the region, the Ministers agreed to the formulation of an ASEAN Cooperation Plan on Trans-boundary Pollution. This Plan initially addresses the following three programme areas:

1. Trans-boundary atmospheric pollution
2. Trans-boundary movement of hazardous wastes
3. Trans-boundary ship-borne pollution

It was recognized that successful implementation of the programme would require public commitment and support.

One of the primary objectives of the trans-boundary atmospheric pollution control programme has been to assess the origin, causes, nature, and extent of local and regional haze incidents. To control the trans-boundary movement of hazardous wastes, it has been agreed that all ASEAN member countries should accede to the Basel Convention. Two measures have been emphasized in this context. The first is the identification of focal points in each ASEAN country; and the second is the exchange of information on the list of hazardous wastes and control procedures on the movement of such wastes as adopted by each country. Finally, it has been made imperative that all ASEAN member countries should develop mechanisms and

### Box 12   Basel Convention

The most comprehensive global environmental agreement on hazardous and other wastes is the Basel Convention on the Control of Trans-boundary Movements of Hazardous Wastes and their Disposal. The Basel Convention came into force in 1992. The Convention has 175 Parties and aims to protect human health and the environment against the adverse effects resulting from the generation, management, trans-boundary movements, and disposal of hazardous and other wastes.

The Convention places a general prohibition on the exportation or importation of wastes between Parties and non-Parties. The exception to this rule is where the waste is subject to another treaty that does not take away from the Basel Convention. The United States is a notable non-Party to the Convention and has a number of such agreements for allowing the shipping of hazardous wastes to Basel Party countries. Article 4 of the Basel Convention requires an overall reduction of waste generation by encouraging countries to *keep wastes within their boundaries and as close as possible to its source of generation*. The Convention explicitly states that illegal hazardous waste traffic is criminal. Yet, it contains no enforcement provisions.

procedures for mitigating pollution caused by ship-borne pollutants.

## Multilateral Environmental Arrangement and Trade Measures

To address the policy coordination problems at a supranational level, Multilateral Environmental Arrangements (MEA) have been created among groups of nations. Well over 200 MEAs now exist, with memberships varying from a relatively small group to over 180 countries covering almost the entire world. Different MEAs cover different aspects of environmental degradation. The main global MEAs that are designed to protect the atmosphere include the 1979 UN Economic Commission for Europe (UNECE) Convention on Long-Range Trans-boundary Air Pollution (together with five protocols on particular pollutants: nitrogen oxides, volatile organic compounds, sulphur, heavy metals, and persistent organic pollutants); the 1985 Vienna Convention for the Protection of the Ozone Layer; the 1987 Montreal Protocol on Substances that Deplete the Ozone Layer; and the 1992 UN framework Convention on Climate

Change, and its protocol, the Kyoto Protocol. The MEAs that cover biodiversity and wildlife include the 1946 International Convention for the Regulation of Whaling; the 1971 Ramsar Convention on Wetlands of International Importance; the 1973 Convention on International Trade in Endangered Species (CITES). The 1998 Rotterdam Convention on the Prior Informed Consent Procedure for Certain Hazardous Chemicals and Pesticides in International Trade and the 2001 Stockholm Convention on Persistent Organic Pollutants, on the other hand, regulate the use of chemicals. Both these MEAs have been agreed upon but are not yet in force. The Montreal Protocol can also be considered under this category since it regulates the production and consumption of ozone-depleting chemicals. Finally, the 1989 Basel Convention on the Control of Trans-boundary Movements of Hazardous Wastes and their Disposal deal with wastes (see Box 12). MEAs appear to be a dynamic and rapidly evolving body of international law. MEAs often include trade measures to enforce the environmental arrangements.

By the Montreal Protocol, countries are required to control consumption and production plus net imports of ozone-depleting substances. As Brack and Gray

(2003) observe, inclusion of net imports in the production definition creates scope for the countries to impose restrictions on trade, including voluntary agreements, taxes, and import bans. Another way trade measures act as instruments for enforcement of multilateral environmental arrangements is the provision of trade prohibition with countries, non-Parties and Parties to MEA alike, which do not comply with MEA. This measure is directly aimed at addressing the coordination problem. Since complying with MEA involves costs, a country may be inclined to avoid them by not implementing some of the policy requirements and thereby gaining unfair comparative advantage vis-à-vis the parties that comply with it. For example, this category of trade measures is built into the *CITES* (see Box 13). *It states that trade with non-parties is prohibited if there is no documentation equivalent to CITES permit. As per estimate of* Brack and Gray (2003), till 2000 CITES trade bans have been imposed on 37 countries. Interestingly, in almost all these cases, the offending country had acceded to the Convention.

Reviewing the effectiveness of trade measures in the CITES, the Montreal Convention, and the Basel Convention, the OECD (1999) concluded that these

**Box 13**   The Convention on International Trade in
Endangered Species (CITES)

CITES, in force since July 1975, is a voluntary international agreement between governments of 175
countries that aims to ensure that international trade
in specimens of wild animals and plants does not
threaten their survival. CITES was drafted as a result
of a resolution adopted in 1963, at a meeting of members of The World Conservation Union. The text of
the Convention was finally agreed upon, at a meeting
of representatives of 80 countries in Washington DC,
USA, on 3 March 1973.

CITES is legally binding on the Parties and provides
a framework to be respected by each Party, which has
to adopt its own domestic legislation to ensure that
the policy framework of CITES is implemented at the
national level.

measures can indeed be effective tools for enforcing
multilateral environmental arrangements, provided, of
course, the parties agree to collectively control international trade as a cause of environmental damage.

# References

## Chapter 1

Acharyya, R. (2001), 'Southern Exports of Dirty Varieties and Optimality of Environmental Regulations: Case of Consumption Externality', paper presented at the conference on *Greater China and WTO*, City University of Hong Kong.

Mani, M. and David Wheeler (1998), 'In Search of Pollution Havens? Dirty Industry in the World Economy, 1960–1995', *Journal of Environment and Development*, 7(3): 215–47.

Ricardo, D. (1817), *The Principles of Political Economy and Taxation*. Reprinted in 1971. New York: Penguin Books.

Sen, A. (2007), 'Linkages between Trade and Environment: Some Analytical Issues', PhD Dissertation, Jadavpur University, Kolkata.

# Chapter 2

Antweiler, W., B.R. Copeland, and M.S. Taylor (2001), 'Is Free Trade Good for the Environment?', *American Economic Review,* 91(4): 877–908.

Bhagwati, J.N. and T.N. Srinivasan (1996), 'Trade and the Environment: Does Environmental Diversity Detract from the Case for Free Trade?', in J. Bhagwati and R.E. Hudec (eds), *Fair Trade and Harmonization: Economic Analysis, Volume 1.* Cambridge: MIT Press, pp. 159–224.

Birdsall, Nancy and David Wheeler (1993), 'Trade Policy and Industrial Pollution in Latin America: Where are the Pollution Havens?', *Journal of Environment and Development,* 2(1): 137–49.

Chattopadhyay, S. (2005), 'Dirtier Trade for India? Story of Globalization', *Contemporary Issues and Ideas in Social Sciences,* November, 1(3): 1–24.

Coase, R. (1960), 'The Problem of Social Cost', *Journal of Law and Economics,* 3: 1–44.

Copeland, B.R. and M.S. Taylor (1999), 'Trade, Spatial Separation, and the Environment', *Journal of International Economics,* 47: 137–68.

————— (2003), 'Trade, Growth and the Environment', NBER Working Paper 9823, National Bureau of Economic Research, Cambridge, MA.

Frankel, J.A. and A.K. Rose (2005), 'Is Trade Good or Bad for the Environment? Sorting Out the Causality?', *The Review of Economics and Statistics,* 87(1): 85–91.

Gamper-Rabindran, S. and S. Jha (2004), 'Environmental Impact of India's Trade Liberalization', paper presented at the '75 Years of Development Conference', Cornell University, May.

Johnson, H.G. (1965), 'Optimal Trade Interventions in the Presence of Domestic Distortions', in R.E. Baldwin et al., *Trade Growth and the Balance of Payments: Essays in Honour of Gottfried Haberler.* Chicago: Rand McNally, pp. 3-34.

Lucas, Robert, David Wheeler, and Hemamala Hettige (1992), 'Economic Development, Environmental Regulation, and the International Migration of Toxic Industrial Pollution, 1960–1988', in Patrick Low (ed.), *International Trade and the Environment.* Washington, DC: World Bank, pp. 67–86.

Mani, M. and D. Wheeler (1998), 'In Search of Pollution Havens? Dirty Industry in the World Economy, 1960–1995', *Journal of Environment and Development*, 7(3): 215–47.

Pigou, A.C. (1912), *Wealth and Welfare*. London: Macmillan.

Rock, M. (1996), 'Pollution Intensity of GDP and Trade Policy: Can the World Bank be Wrong?', *World Development*, 24(3): 471–9.

## Chapter 3

Aditya, A. and R. Acharyya (2011), 'Export Diversification, Composition and Economic Growth: Evidence from

Cross-Country Analysis', *Journal of International Trade and Economic Development*, pp. 1–34.

Andreoni, James and Arik Levinson (2000), 'The Simple Analytics of the Environmental Kuznets Curve', *Journal of Public Economics*, 80: 269–86.

Cole, M.A. (2003), 'Development, Trade and the Environment: How Robust is the Environmental Kuznets Curve?', *Environment and Development Economics*, 8(4): 555–80.

Cole, M.A., A.J. Rayner, and J.M. Bates (1997), 'Environmental Kuznets Curve: An Empirical Analysis', *Environment and Development Economics*, 2: 410–16.

Cole, M.A. and E. Neumayer (2005), 'Environmental Policy and the Environmental Kuznets Curve: Can Developing Countries Escape the Detrimental Consequences of Economic Growth?', in P. Dasgupta (ed.), *International Handbook of Environmental Policies*. Cheltenham, UK and Northampton, MA, USA: Edward Elgar, pp. 298–318.

Copeland, B.R. and M.S. Taylor (1994), 'North–South Trade and the Environment', *Quarterly Journal of Economics*, 109: 755–87.

——— (2003), 'Trade, Growth and the Environment', NBER Working Paper 9823, National Bureau of Economic Research, Cambridge, MA.

Dasgupta, P., B. Laplante, H. Wang, and D. Wheeler (2002), 'Confronting the Environmental Kuznets Curve', *Journal of Economic Perspectives,* 16(1): 147–68.

Dean, J.M. (2002), 'Does Trade Liberalization Harm the Environment? A New Test', *Canadian Journal of Economics*, 35: 819–42.

Dean, J. and M.E. Lovely (2008), 'Trade Growth, Production Fragmentation and China's Environment', NBER Working Paper 13860, Cambridge, MA.

Dinda, S. (2004), 'Environmental Kuznets Curve Hypothesis: A Survey', *Ecological Economics,* 49: 431–55.

Dollar, D. and A. Kraay (2001), 'Trade, Growth and Poverty', Policy Research Working Paper 2199.

Frankel, J. and D. Romer (1999), 'Does Trade Cause Growth?', *American Economic Review*, 89(3): 379–99.

Grossman, G. and E. Helpman (1991), *Innovation and Growth in the Global Economy*. Cambridge, MA: MIT Press.

Grossman, Gene M. and Alan B. Krueger (1993), 'Environmental Impacts of a North American Free Trade Agreement', in P. Garber (ed.), *The U.S.–Mexico Free Trade Agreement*. Cambridge, MA: MIT Press, pp. 13–56.

Grossman, G.M. and A.O. Krueger (1995), 'Economic Growth and the Environment', *The Quarterly Journal of Economics*, May, 110(2): 353–77.

Hausmann, R., J. Hwang, and Dani Rodrik (2007), 'What You Export Matters', *Journal of Economic Growth*, 12(1): 1–25.

Hettige, H., R.E.B. Lucas, and D. Wheeler (1992), 'The Toxic Intensity of Industrial Production: Global Patterns, Trends and Trade Policy', *American Economic Review*, 82(2): 478–81.

Hettige, H., M. Mani, and D. Wheeler (2000), 'Industrial Pollution in Economic Development: Kuznets Revisited', *Journal of Development Economics*, 62: 445–76.

Kuznets, S. (1955), 'Economic Growth and Income Inequality', *American Economic Review*, 45: 1–28.

Matsuura, K. and F. Takeda (2005), 'Trade and the Environment in East Asia: Examining the Linkages with Japan and the USA', paper presented at the 2005 Meeting of the Midwest Economics Association, USA.

Rodriguez, F. and D. Rodrik (1999), 'Trade Policy and Economic Growth: A Skeptic's Guide to Cross-National Evidence', NBER Working Paper W7081, Cambridge, MA.

Rodrik, D. (2006), 'What's so Special about China's Exports?', NBER Working Paper 11947, Cambridge, MA.

Rybczynski, T.N. (1955), 'Factor Endowment and Relative Commodity Prices', *Economica*, 12: 336–41.

Selden, T.M. and D. Song (1994), 'Environmental Quality and Development: Is there a Kuznets Curve for Air Pollution Emissions?', *Journal of Environmental Economics and Management*, 27: 147–62.

Stolper, W. and P.A. Samuelson (1941), 'Protection and Real Wages', *Review of Economic Studies*, 9: 58–73.

# Chapter 4

Acharyya, J. (2009), 'FDI, Growth and the Environment: Evidence from India on $CO_2$ Emissions during the Last

Two Decades', *Journal of Economic Development*, 34(1): 43–57.

Adams, J. (1997), 'Environmental Policy and Competitiveness in a Globalized Economy: Conceptual Issues and a Review of Empirical Evidences', in *OECD, Globalization and Environment: Preliminary Perspectives.* Paris: OECD, pp. 53–100.

Baek, J. and W.W. Koo (2008), 'A Dynamic Approach to the FDI–Environment Nexus: The Case of China and India', paper presented at the 2008 Annual Meeting of the American Agricultural Economics Association, Orlando, Florida.

Borregaard, N., A. Dufey, and L. Winchester (2008), 'Effects of Foreign Investment versus Domestic Investment on the Forestry Sector in Latin America (Chile and Brazil): Demystifying FDI Effects Related to the Environment'. Discussion Paper # 15, The Working Group on Development and Environment in the Americas.

Dean, J. and M.E. Lovely (2008), 'Trade Growth, Production Fragmentation and China's Environment', NBER Working Paper 13860, Cambridge, MA.

Dean, J., M.E. Lovely, and H. Wang (2004), 'Foreign Direct Investment and Pollution Havens: Evaluating the Evidence from China', US International Trade Commission Working Paper 2004–01-B.

Eskeland, G.S. and A.E. Harrison (2003), 'Moving to Greener Pastures? Multinationals and the Pollution

Haven Hypothesis?', *Journal of Development Economics*, 70(1): 1–23.

Haltia, O. and K. Keipi (2000), 'Financiamiento De Inversiones Forestales En América Latina: El Uso De Incentivos', in Kari Keipi (ed.), *Políticas Forestales En América Latina*. Washington DC, USA: Banco Interamericano de Desarrollo.

Jaffe, A., S. Peterson, P. Portney, and R. Stavins (1995), 'Environmental Regulation and the Competitiveness of U.S. Manufacturing: What Does the Evidence Tell Us?', *The Journal of Economic Literature*, 33: 132–63.

Luce, D. and H. Raiffa (1957), *Games and Decisions: Introduction and Critical Survey*. New York: John Wily & Sons., Inc.

Mani, M. and David Wheeler (1998), 'In Search of Pollution Havens? Dirty Industry in the World Economy, 1960–1995', *Journal of Environment and Development*, 7(3): 215–47.

OECD (2002), 'Environmental Issues in Policy-based Competition for Investment: A Literature Review', OECD, Paris.

Smarzynska, B. and Wei Shang-Jin (2004), 'Pollution Havens and Foreign Direct Investment: Dirty Secret or Popular Myth?', *Contributions to Economic Analysis & Policy*, 3(2).

UNCTAD (2003), *World Investment Report 2003*. Geneva: UNCTAD.

Xing, Y. and C. Kolstad (2002), 'Do Lax Environmental Regulations Attract Foreign Investment?', *Environmental and Resource Economics*, 21(1): 1–22.

Zarsky, L. (1999), 'Havens, Halos and Spaghetti: Untangling the Evidence about Foreign Direct Investment and the Environment', in *Foreign Direct Investment and the Environment*. Paris: OECD, pp. 47–74.

# Chapter 5

Akbostancý, E., G. Ýpek Tunç, and Serap Türüt-A°ýk (2004), 'Pollution Haven Hypothesis and the Role of Dirty Industries in Turkey's Exports', ERC Working Paper 04/03.

Antweiler, W., B.R. Copeland, and M.S. Taylor (2001), 'Is Free Trade Good for the Environment?', *American Economic Review*, 91: 877–908.

Bhagwati, J.N., and T.N. Srinivasan (1996), 'Trade and the Environment: Does Environmental Diversity Detract from the Case for Free Trade?', in J. Bhagwati and R.E. Hudec (eds), *Fair Trade and Harmonization: Economic Analysis*, Volume 1, Cambridge, MA: MIT Press.

Chichilnisky, G. (1994), 'Global Environment and North–South Trade', *American Economic Review*, 84: 851–74.

Copeland, B.R. and M.S. Taylor (1994), 'North–South Trade and the Environment', *Quarterly Journal of Economics*, 109: 755–87.

——— (2003), 'Trade, Growth and the Environment', NBER Working Paper No. 9823.

Grossman, G. and A. Krueger (1993), 'Environmental Impacts of a North American Free Trade Agreement', in P. Garber (ed.), *The US–Mexico Free Trade Agreement*. Cambridge: MIT Press.

Mani, M. and David Wheeler (1998), 'In Search of Pollution Havens? Dirty Industry in the World Economy, 1960–1995', *Journal of Environment and Development*, 7(3): 215–47.

Pethig, R. (1976), 'Pollution, Welfare, and Environmental Policy in the Theory of Comparative Advantage', *Journal of Environmental Economics and Management*, 2: 160–9.

Tobey, J. (1990), 'The Effects of Domestic Environmental Policies on Patterns of World Trade', *Kyklos*, 43(2): 191–209.

van Beers, C. and J.C.J.M. van den Bergh (1997), 'An Empirical Multi-Country Analysis of the Impact of Environmental Regulations on Foreign Trade Flows', *Kyklos*, 50(1): 29–46.

Xu, X. (2000), 'International Trade and Environmental Regulation: Time Series Evidence and Cross Section Test', *Environmental and Resource Economics*, 17: 233–57.

# Chapter 6

Belcher, K. (2007), 'Trade Agreements and Multilateral Environmental Arrangement', in W.A. Kerr and J.D.

Gaisford (eds), *Handbook on International Trade Policy*. UK: Edward Elgar Publishing Limited.

Brack, D. and K. Gray (2003), 'Multilateral Environmental Arrangement and the WTO: Report September 2003', Royal Institute of International Affairs—Sustainable Development Programme, International Institute for Sustainable Development.

Copeland, B. (1996), 'Pollution Content Tariffs, Environmental Rent Shifting and the Control of Cross-Border Pollution', *Journal of International Economics*, 40: 459–76.

Dollar, D. and A. Kraay (2001), 'Trade, Growth and Poverty'. Policy Research Working Paper # 2199, World Bank.

Maler, G. (1992), 'International Environmental Problems', in A. Markandya and J. Richardson (eds), *Environmental Economics*, London: Earthscan Publication Limited.

OECD (1999), *Trade Measures in Multilateral Environmental Agreements*. Paris: OECD.

Sanyal, K. and R. Acharyya (2001), 'The Environmental Issues in A Globalized World: An Overview', in R. Acharyya and B. Moitra (eds), *Effects of Globalization on Industry and Environment*. New Delhi: Lancer's Books.

# Index